# Roving with LaLah

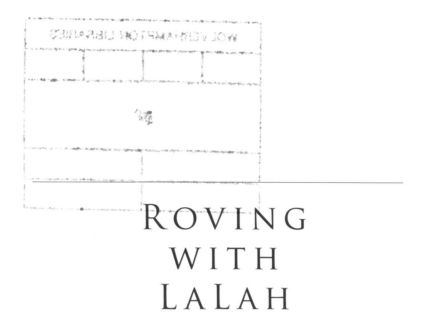

# ROVING WITH LALAH

## SLICES OF EVERYDAY JAMAICAN LIFE

### *Robert Lalah*

*Kingston • Miami*

First published in Jamaica, 2008 by
Ian Randle Publishers
11 Cunningham Avenue
Box 686
Kingston 6
www.ianrandlepublishers.com

Text © 2008, Robert Lalah
Photographs © 2008, The Gleaner Company

ISBN 978-976-637-363-4 (Hardback)

A catalogue record for this book is available from the National Library
of Jamaica

Cover images courtesy of the Jamaica Gleaner
Cover design and book design by Ian Randle Publishers
Printed in China

*For my father Errol and brother Kevin; my source of strength, always.*

# CONTENTS

# FOREWORD

The concept of 'Roving with Lalah' came about during a conversation Robert and I had in my office at The *Gleaner* in September 2005. I had only minutes earlier called all my reporters together to discuss with them the findings of a media survey. One of the findings was that we weren't doing as well in rural areas as we would have liked. Our readership in rural Jamaica wasn't great and many persons from these little, out-of-the-way communities felt that they were being largely ignored by the print media. I called on all my reporters in that meeting to think of ways we could counteract this problem, and others, and to keep thinking outside the box to come up with ideas for features and stories that have never been done before.

About fifteen minutes after the meeting, there's a knock on my office door and in walks Robert. He tells me he has something to run by me. I offer him a seat and the rest, as they say, is history.

The instant success of 'Roving with Lalah' was amazing and quite frankly caught me by surprise. From the publication of the very first feature, I realized that we were on to something big. In came the letters overnight from fans that continue to this day. Every week, we receive several dozen letters that are, in one way or another, in praise of this feature. It did manage to stir up some amount of excitement in rural communities across the country, but the bulk of our readership, came from somewhere a bit unexpected: Jamaicans living abroad. They really latched on immediately and they let us know, really soon, that this was what they had been waiting for, for a long time. 'Roving with Lalah' provides them with a taste of Jamaica as they remember it. It stirs up their memories of home and all of a sudden, the things they know and love of their homeland come alive in their consciousness. Through Robert's writing they travel across the island, hear the voices and distinct dialect of its people, breath, the fresh country air, smell the soil, feel the heat on their skins and for the few minutes it takes them to read the feature each week, they are home. It's obvious from the response alone, that this is no small gift for these members of the Jamaican diaspora, many of whom have been away for decades.

'Roving with Lalah' takes them home whenever they need a piece of 'yard.' I'm proud of what 'Roving with Lalah' has become in a short space of time, especially because of how it all came about; through a conversation. It really is an example to young writers everywhere who have innovative ideas, but may be too intimidated to speak up. 'Roving with Lalah' has quickly become a favourite of people living all over the world and it all started from a chat in an office initiated by the youngest writer on staff at the time.

Garfield Grandison
*Editor-in-Chief*
**The Gleaner Company**

"Well **Mocho is basically what you see here.** There isn't much more. Things are quiet and we all know each other. We don't have anything to worry about, like crime."

A Hearty Game of Dominoes

# MAGNIFICENT MOCHO, CLARENDON

## 'Go Weh! You look like somebody weh come from Mocho!

I remember hearing that once or twice as a child, and always wondered what sort of horn-sprouting, webbed-feet characters must come from a place so ribald. My childhood imagination conjured up images of witches with triangular hats whose mouths would sprout fire at the first glance of a scared young lad such as myself.

So when, in response to your emails, I learned that I would be called upon to venture to the town of my childhood nightmares, I must admit I was overcome with trepidation. But with a reassuring, 'do it or go home' from my editor, I set off to the much maligned Mocho.

Now there are at least two places in Jamaica called Mocho. There's one in St. James near Garlands, but most persons agree that the Mocho from those infamous insults is the tiny town in Clarendon, between Thompson Town and Green Park.

I wondered what to take with me on the trip. Bug spray? Bottled water, or perhaps a crucifix? I had no idea what to expect.

Eventually, off we went; Photographer Ian Allen and myself. After travelling from Kingston for a couple of hours through miles of hilly terrain and bumpy, crater–filled roads, we finally got to the place so slandered. We came across a small cluster of decadent buildings with zinc roofs that were brown with age. This made a colourful picture, especially when coupled with huge green trees and that pesky rural town red dirt. This was Mocho.

We stopped by the side of the road and drew curious stares from a small group of beautiful women standing in the shade of a tree. I stepped out of the car to finally face this place I had wondered about since I was but a lad.

At first I was a bit surprised to see that the town was just like any other rural town. There was the customary rickety old shop in the square, where the barely audible sound coming from a radio was accompanied only by the sound of distant chatter. Otherwise, there was simply silence. It had been a rainy week, so the sky was still full of patches of gumetal-grey clouds.

A few bearded old men sat on wooden stools at the entrance to a bar and you guessed it, they were the lively bunch. They sat sipping from green bottles of beer and hurling profanties in the direction of the miniskirt-wearing belles, who in return for the overtures, sent dirty looks in the direction of the men.

Now as everyone knows, a town is defined by the people who live there. So we went right into the crowd to get to know the people from the town that holds

the dubious honour of being one of the most disparaged communities in Jamaica.

We first met Mavis Stewart, who owns, operates and lives at the back of the most popular shop in town. You know the kind, the shop that sells everything from engine oil to banana chips. The rotund woman had a wide smile and the weight of her rather rounded derriere seemed to slow her down as she led us into the shop.

This kind middle-aged woman offered us seats and described life in this sleepy old town. 'Well Mocho is basically what you see here. There isn't much more. Things are quiet and we all know each other. We don't have anything to worry about, like crime. So whatever anybody want to say about Mocho, that is their problem. We are all quite alright,' the perky woman grinned. Others simply laughed when we asked how they felt about their town being the butt of so many jokes. One toothless, white-haired bloke said he was

One of many rustic buildings in Mocho

proud to be from Mocho, because it was the most famous town in Jamaica.

The young people however, tend to shy away from letting on that they are from Mocho. At school, when asked, they prefer to say they are from Four Paths or Thompson Town. But what do the people of this quaint little town do for fun? Well, there isn't much to do, to be honest. Most people laughed at the question and said they would meet up at the bar and drink and eat, but that was pretty much all there was to do. For anything else, they would hop on a bus to Four Paths or even as far away as May Pen. There was one fellow who gave a different answer when asked what the towns people do for fun, but that was a tad too blunt for this medium.

We eventually stumbled on to a heated game of dominoes well in progress. It was like a festival of profanity as these self-proclaimed 'country people' enjoyed themselves in the best way they know how. One man got a bit excited and threw his hands into the air and ordained himself the domino King of Mocho. But a whisper from a female bartender confirmed that it was just the alcohol talking.

As we walked further into the community, we met several children, all of whom were quick to say their 'good mornings' before passing us by. There was a group of boys playing marbles and a couple of girls playing under a tree. All of them were quick to greet us with wide, bright smiles. Refreshing.

At the police station, a building in serious need of repair, we met Dian Fairweather, who before even finding out our names, offered to cook us dinner. These Mocho people - they really are different.

The biggest problem these laid-back country folk say they have, is that there hasn't been any significant development in the community for years. With the stigma often attached to the area, many persons simply wait for the first opportunity to leave. The end result of that, is an ageing town with a dwindling population. The residents say they're worried that eventually there will be nothing left and the community will just fade away with the times.

But despite that, the Mocho people say they are happy and love their town, no matter what anybody says. So after spending most of the day in the quaint little community, I have to admit, it really was hard to leave. The residents were so friendly that I felt as if I had made a community of new friends. At last, my childhood fears were finally put to rest.

So next time someone tells you that you look like someone from Mocho, just smile and say thank you, because it really is a great compliment.

---

*Note: To Patricia who lives in the house behind the bar: Again, I'm sorry, I just didn't have the time...but call me!*

# SPICY
# MIDDLE QUARTERS

Perlitta lifted the cover from the blackened dutch pot and used a giant leaf to fan the flames underneath.

She shifted a log that was under the pot and a puff of white smoke rose to her eyes. She started to squint, but as a car whizzed by, Perlitta's eyes lit up. 'Swims here. Hot peppa swims here!' Zoom! And the car was gone.

'Bwoy if I know you was coming, I woulda tidy up di place likkle,' Perlitta said as she dumped the contents of the pot into a plastic container on the makeshift table in front of her.

I looked around and wondered just what there was to be tidied up. After all, as far as I could see, there was just bush, dirt and a sorry-looking dog there beside her. I guess she must have seen me looking around quizzically, so Perlitta spoke up. 'Mi woulda did sweep up di place likkle and thing,' she said.

But there on the roadside in the quiet community, I couldn't have asked for a better reception. You see, photographer Norman Grindley and I had not been in Middle Quarters, St. Elizabeth for more than a minute

Middle Quarters, St. Elizabeth

before we were approached by the friendly Perlitta, carrying a batch of her famous peppered shrimp. Yes, Middle Quarters is known across the island as the shrimp capital of Jamaica and the second we got there, we figured out why.

Lining the streets from the sign that says 'Welcome to Middle Quarters', to as far as the eyes could see, were dozens of women, children and even a few men waving the little red creatures at passing motorists.

Perlitta was one of the first in the line.

'Yes sar. I been here fi more than 16 years. I use di likkle swims money and put mi pickney dem into school. Is not much, but what di good Lord bless you with you must be grateful for,' she said as she stirred something in the pot.

'Me and mi likkle dutch pot been doing fine,' she beamed as she spoke. Now Perlitta is by no means a modest shrimp cook. No sir, to hear her tell it, her peppered shrimps are beyond compare.

'Yes man. Is all about knowing the right amount of pepper and salt. For if you ration di peppa, den it nah go come out right,' she said, a serious look in her eyes.

So how much will the best shrimp in the country set you back? Well, not necessarily as much as you might expect. Perlitta's eyes widened and she started to rub her stomach when I asked her this.

'Look yah man. We is all one people around here. We sell by conscience. Sometime people stop and dem say that dem don't have more than $50 so we only sell them that amount. And sometime some school pickney come and nuh have more than $20, so we sell dem that amount. We just use we conscience,' she explained.

Soon, a small van drove up with two men on board and Perlitta ran up to them with her container of fresh shrimp. We bid her farewell and went off deeper into the community. A slim, ageing woman wearing a cap was sitting on a chair under a tree with a bucket at her feet. She barely

smiled as we approached her and told her of our business in the community.

She looked us up and down and after about two minutes, she said, 'So unnu not buying any swims?'

After a few niceties, the woman soon came around. Everyone calls her Miss Vie and she has been selling shrimp in Middle Quarters for more than 25 years. She is one of the more popular vendors in the community. 'Mi deh yah since Wappie kill Phillup and all when him dead and come back I will still be here,' she said. We asked Miss Vie to tell us about life in Middle Quarters.

'It easy going. I remember when I was a girl, dis place used to carry the swing. Dem time deh jukebox was just coming in and I used to go drop legs at di shop. But I am a Christian now, mi nuh badda wid dat again. But it woulda nice if somebody play a jukebox again though. Mi can't dance to it, but at least mi coulda move mi foot. For Jesus don't love when you too deady deady,' she chuckled as she spoke.

Miss Vie spotted a woman walking on the opposite side of the road. 'Sherrel! Come yah young gyal! Come

chat to di man dem!' she shouted and the woman sauntered over. 'Hello please,' the woman said. We asked her how the shrimp business was going. 'Well right now it kinda poko poko. But other time it alright. Is what we round here do fi a living,' said Sherrel, smiling.

So what do the hard working people of Middle Quarters do for fun? 'Well if dem bring back a jukebox inna di square den it woulda nice up back tings. At least mi coulda move mi foot to some music,' said Miss Vie, much to the amusement of Sherrel and a few other women standing nearby.

'Is what you laughing about? We need back a jukebox! We need fi get some long hair Chiney fi come open up a shop and nice up di place,' Miss Vie was adamant. 'Things was nicer when mi was a girl, a true unnu nuh know!' Miss Vie continued and the others kept on laughing. Soon it was time for us to be off again, so we said goodbye to the shrimp people of Middle Quarters and with a smile and a wave, they wished us well.

Miss Vie said, 'Walk good and may God go with you. When you a drive nuh badda stop and take up nobody. Just go straight home! Until a nedda time again!'

# SCARY MINIBUS RIDE

For reasons that now seem incomprehensible, I decided a couple days ago to hop on a bus from Spanish Town to Old Harbour in St. Catherine. That was one fleeting moment of insanity on my part and it is with great appreciation for my survival that I reflect on the events of that day.

It all started sometime close to midday when I walked up to a sign with the words 'Bus Stop' on Burke Road in the heart of Spanish Town. There were two men and a woman already standing there. One of the men was dressed in a long-sleeved shirt and a pair of what looked like green velvet trousers. He had a large bag in his hand and kept glancing anxiously at his watch. The other fellow was more casual, in a T-shirt, short pants and sandals that, in my estimation, exposed too much of an unfortunate pair

of feet. The woman seemed upset and crinkled her nose as a bead of sweat ran down her cheek. She was not much more than five feet tall and was at least one hundred pounds overweight.

'Good morning,' I said in a cheery voice.

'Urgh,' was the response from the bag-carrier. The woman turned to me, looked me over and just went back to staring down the road with a vexed look on her face. The sandal-wearer didn't even glance in my direction. I was in quite a bit of hurry, so when the first bus pulled up, even though I had serious reservations, I decided to take the risk. Now, I should point out that the first bus that pulled up was a white and blue minibus that screeched in front of us quite unexpectedly. It stirred up a cloud of dust and that, coupled with the thick black smoke coming from the exhaust pipe, made for an uncomfortable few seconds. The bus had a sticker that read 'Original Contender' on the windscreen. On the back were the words 'Original Rude Boy'.

A dark-skinned man in an even darker pair of sunglasses was hanging from the door at the side of the bus. He was wearing a white merino and a pair of jeans.

'Ole Harba, Ole Harba!' he shouted, still dangling from the bus. My two companions did not hesitate. They jumped into the bus and quickly squeezed into two of only a few empty seats. I was a bit more reluctant, but a tart reprimand from the bespectacled conductor hastened my steps. 'Yow hurry up nuh man!' So into the bus I went. It was a tiny thing with garbage on the floor. There were, perhaps, nine other people on the bus and they all seemed upset for some reason. Before I could find my way to an empty seat, the bus driver gunned the engine. We rocked back and forth for a while and I finally found a bit of space to sit beside a woman in a long, red skirt and track shoes.

'Hello,' I said. No response. I realised quickly that I would get nowhere with her, so I looked around the bus to entertain myself. Across from me sat a boy in a khaki shirt and trousers. He was digging greedily into a bag of banana chips and seemed rather amused with me. He kept staring at me and chuckling at what I imagine, was my obvious discomfort.

The bus conductor with the dark glasses now sat quietly at the doorway. Even though inside the bus was extremely dark, he made no move toward removing the spectacles. I chuckled out loud as I looked over at him and he turned and stared straight at me. This muffled my laughter rather quickly and I hastily looked in the other direction. On the other side of me was an elderly bloke who seemed friendly enough. He was wearing a brown shirt with matching pants and black shoes. A rather snazzy dresser. 'Good morning,' I said. 'Hello mi son. How you do?' he said. I was pleasantly surprised by his demeanour. He told me his name was Franky. I asked Franky if he had taken this particular bus before. 'Bwoy, mi nuh memba. Di whole a dem look di same to me. Mi live a Old Harbour Bay and mi only come a Spanish Town fi look fi mi daughter. When time mi come mi nuh too tarry, for dem bus man yah drive hard when it come to night time. Mi like do what mi doing and leave out early for mi nuh able fi go crash inna nuh bus,' he said. Franky had only a few teeth, but opened his mouth wide when he smiled. The bus took a sharp turn and the lot of us all leaned to the left. 'Dem drive hard you see man,' Franky said. I nodded my head in agreement, much to the amusement of the boy with the banana chips.

The angry looking woman in the sneakers made a hissing sound with her mouth. 'Driva tek time nuh man. Wah do you?' she shouted.

'Hey, kip quiet! A di pothole dem. You want mi fi drop inna it and buss up mi tyre?' the driver retorted, looking up at his rear view mirror.

'Mi nuh business wid you and yuh tyre. Just tek time wid me,' the woman shouted back. Franky giggled. I cracked a smile, but then noticed the conductor staring at me through his thick dark glasses. He did not seem happy. I quickly changed my smile into a cough so as to not anger him further.

'One stop!' shouted someone from the back. The bus screeched to a sudden halt and we all rocked forward. My head hit the seat in front of me and the woman sitting there turned and gave me a nasty look. The person who shouted for the driver to stop was a young woman wearing a pink wig and yellow shoes. As she exited the bus, the conductor whispered something to her. 'Tek you nasty self outa mi way! You head fava bull frog!' the woman shouted to him as she stepped out. I burst out laughing until the conductor turned around and looked at me again through his creepy sunglasses. I sobered up. Soon we were off again. Franky said he preferred taking taxis, but there were times he had to just catch a bus heading in his direction. 'Sometime you haffi rush you hear. Ah nuh all di time you have di money fi tek taxi neither,' he said.

To my great relief, I looked out the window and realised that we were approaching Old Harbour. The bus made a sudden stop and again we all jolted forward. As I hopped out and said goodbye to Franky, I glanced back at the bus and saw the bespectacled conductor still staring at me though his creepy dark sunglasses.

# NINE MILES, ST. ANN

So here's the scoop on Rhoden Hall in St. Ann as told to me by residents about a week ago. Sonia is convinced that someone stole her cellphone, even though she doesn't remember where she had it last or how long ago it went missing. Her neighbours are convinced that the only thing she has lost is her mind, and are trying to discourage her from going ahead with her plans to call the local television stations to, as she put it 'mek di dutty tief dem know mi a come fi dem.'

Meanwhile, Winston, the yam farmer, is getting a bit tired of carrying water on his head to use in his field and is seriously considering running some pipes to make life easier. But that kind of highfalutin thinking only got him laughed at.

Rhoden Hall is a little place in St. Ann where there still is no running water and where everyone still knows each other's name. Never heard of Rhoden Hall? Well, maybe you know it by its more well known title, Nine Miles. Yes, its the very same Nine Miles where reggae legend Bob Marley once ran around in diapers. When he was a baby, of course.

Someone told me that about 500 tourists from places I've never even heard of visit the community everyday. That just blew me away. I mean, to think that people still flock to this tiny place just to feel closer to the reggae star. Then I started wondering about the other people who live in Nine Miles. I mean, what's their story? Everyone associates the name of the community with the deceased singer, and you really never hear anything about the people who live there now. So that was the intention when photographer Norman Grindley and I set out for Nine Miles. We wanted to find out what else was happening in the community other than tourists visiting the Marley mausoleum. Note to self: Next time you think of going to Nine Miles, don't have such a big breakfast, you'll regret it. It's such a winding road, I almost got dizzy, twice. We passed places like Prickle Pole and St. Ann's Bay.

Eventually, we got there; it must have been about midday. The first thing we came across that hinted to us that we were in Nine Miles, was a huge sign painted on a wall that read 'You are now

(c) 2006 The Gleaner Co.

in Nine Miles'. I guess it might have been more than a hint.

A burly, dark-skinned man sporting a huge gold chain around his neck and even more gold in his mouth, was standing next to a large concrete wall. Just above the wall was a sign that read 'Bob Marley Mausoleum'. We parked the van and hopped out. By the way, the air up there in the hills is like heaven to the lungs. Although there was a hint of a certain potent ... ah ... bush in the air. But I guess that was to be expected.

'Need a tour mon?' inquired the bejewelled bloke. When we responded with: 'No bredrin, we jus' a pass through,' the man's dialect made a snap adjustment and he said, 'Oh, zeen mi bredda.'

He gave his name as Donald, and seemed quite

confused when we told him we weren't there to visit the Bob Marley mausoleum, but instead wanted to find out about the community. 'Mi ah ... you sure you nuh want a tour?' he asked with a most puzzled look on his face.

Eventually, Donald came around and told us that the townspeople really were largely ignored. 'Nothing much happen around here. Everything really quiet still. Everybody just take it easy.'

We bid the man farewell and went down a slope to meet a few people we saw standing together. It was here that we met the very vocal Sonia. She is a dark-skinned woman of medium build. She was wearing a blue and white dress and sitting between two men with strikingly muddy shoes.

'You want to know about Nine Miles? A dutty tief move wid mi phone and him ago pay fi it. Mi ago work pan dem till dem bring back mi phone!' Sonia's monologue brought her companions to a hearty chuckle. But with one mean glance, the irate woman silenced her hecklers.

'Is $3,000 mi pay fi mi phone and mi a go get it back!' she said. While Sonia sat mumbling something about a certain bush she was going to use to get back at the phone thief, the men around her said there wasn't much to Nine Miles other than its link to the

reggae legend. 'Bwoy it quiet still. I guess that good 'cause the people live loving still. But if you want likkle enjoyment you haffi go somewhere else,' said Milton who wore dark sunglasses in the shade.

We were told that most of the persons in the community were farmers and enjoyed a quiet, simple life.

There were a lot of children running around and tour buses kept entering and leaving the mausoleum. In fact, for the few hours we were in the community, about 15 buses full of caucasion finger pointers in tie-and-dye ensembles came and went. Curious bunch. We noticed a few persons standing casually along the roadway that leads to the mausoleum. Someone told us to keep an eye on them and we would find out how most of the residents survive. We did this for a while, but nothing happened. Suddenly, someone shouted 'Tourist a come!' and it was like a fox hunt had been heralded.

Children came out of every corner of the community, some with plates of food still in their hands and ran in the direction from which the shout came. Two chubby white women wearing Bob Marley t-shirts and a boy in a red, green and gold shirt and hat were making their way slowly up the hill. They had wide smiles on their faces and seemed happy to be greeted by the crowd of locals.

One wrinkled man gave the official welcome. 'Hello mon. Wecome to Bab Morley town. If you want a smoke we gots it for you. If you want a drink, we gots that too. Let us know, anything you needs. Make sure you know we is here to please,' he said, to the tourists who didn't seem to understand a word.

As we were watching this painful display, a man wearing boots and carrying a machete approached us. 'Hello please, what you doing please?' he inquired timidly. We found out his name was Winston, a proud yam farmer. He said he enjoyed the easy-going lifestyle of Nine Miles, but said he had a serious problem. 'Bwoy mi tired fi carry water. Mi back tired now. Plus di likkle donkey mi have a get old, suh mi think mi a go try line up some pipe fi miself,' he said, using his hands to shield his eyes from the sun. We also met Sharon who works in a bar across from the mausoleum. She said that if people wanted to know about the real Nine Miles, all they had to do was visit. 'We all love when people visit. Everybody welcome and everybody safe,' she said. So our time in the famous community came to an end all too quickly. We had such a good time and realised that there was so much more to Nine Miles than people realise.

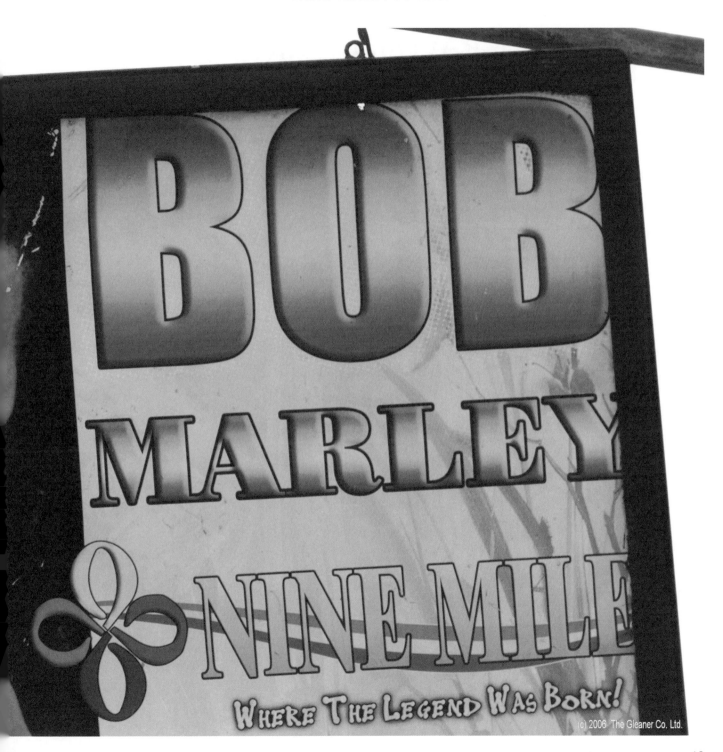

# GRAVESIDE PARTY IN NONSUCH

When anyone I know gets together with friends, it's normally to have fun and engage in a chaotic episode of general debauchery. It happens more often than I'd like to admit here. For employment purposes.

Up to recently, I thought there was no party like a Kingston party. But on a lonely road in the hills of Portland, I came across a sleepy little district, where the fun and revelry is unlike anything I'd experienced before. There, the festivities take place only when someone dies. Yes, when someone dies.

You see, photographer Norman Grindley and I were on a voluntary wild goose chase. We weren't sure exactly where we were going, but were intent on finding an interesting town somewhere. We headed east, with Portland on our minds.

Things started out quite pleasant, but after a while, it seemed there was nothing going on, nothing to see in East Portland. Eventually, after being crammed in that automobile for more than two hours, with each of us harbouring similar homicidal thoughts for the other, we struck a gold mine.

We had passed through Reach, drove through Kensington, up Zion Hill, pass Sherwood Forest, and were on a stretch of road with nothing but trees and bush on both sides. After not seeing any sign of life for what seemed like forever, we went around a bend and suddenly found ourselves facing a huge crowd. There were people everywhere. The crowd spilled over into a small graveyard right by the side of the road. Some stood in the roadway, some under a tree and others further off, seemingly working in the graveyard. We asked a man who was standing by the side of the road just where were we.

'This is Nonsuch. There is no such place!' he grinned.

Nonsuch is a tiny district of no more than 600 residents. We were told that there were two towns called Nonsuch in Portland, but this one also goes by the moniker of 'Lookout'.

'What's happening? Why the crowd?' I asked.

'It's a grave digging,' was the reply.

'Come outa di van, man. You nuh see seh a bashment! Mi need help.'

We were puzzled by this statement. But then, the smiling man pointed to two curvy girls standing beside him. 'Mi need help. Too much for me alone,' he chuckled. We dived out of the vehicle. You don't have to tell us twice.

The man, we later found out, goes by the title 'G Unit'. We followed his trail into the 'High Vibes' bar. There were three dreadlocked men inside, holding bottles of dragon stout and cups containing a clear pungent liquid. They were sporting very dark sunglasses and seemed happy. High spirited, if you will. We could get nothing coherent from them, so we turned to the bartender; a tall, lanky dreadlocked man of Indian descent. He's Delroy King.

'That's how you celebrate grave digging?' we enquired.

'That is how the whole town do it. We all come together whenever somebody dies and cook food, drink liquor and hold a vibes, while we dig the grave. Nobody pays for anything and everybody

chip in.' Delroy was supplying free liquor to everyone. Others had taken green bananas from their fields, some brought flour and others, meat. Those who couldn't afford to take anything, well, they became the official grave diggers.

A group of women, all chatting loudly, were gathered under a tree at the far corner of the graveyard, cooking. They were bent over huge bubbling pots of food, stirring what seemed like soup, with long metal spoons.

We went over to them. The smell of the soup was strong enough to knock you over. Patricia

King was the head cook for the day. Before I even introduced myself to her, she said, 'Drink soup. You have to drink soup,' handing me a steaming cup. After a timid inquisition on my part, I found out that it was goat head soup. God help me. Not my idea of a hearty meal. But I took the cup and did the best I could. I'm paying for that even today.

A group of children sat nearby, and their eyes widened with excitement as Mr. Grindley snapped pictures.

Further up the hill, two old men were in a heated debate

about the afterlife. They were both holding beer bottles. Not the same bottles we saw them with when we just got there, so this made for some colourful language.

I thanked the women for the soup and walked off.

I met Stedford Latouche, a dark-skinned man, about 30 years old. I took a sip of the soup, and with a grimace, asked him if they had any trouble with crime in the community.

'Nothing like that. We all live good. Look around. This is all of us right here. Or most. You can do anything. Leave your car open and it will alright,' he said. Delroy the bartender, who had rejoined us, spoke up.

'We nuh do dem ting deh. Crime and dem ting deh. We just live till we dead. Then we celebrate.'

We found out that the woman who they were digging the grave for, was well respected and had died of natural causes. Her husband, Beresford King, was among a group of men chatting by the side of the road. We walked with him toward the grave site.

I asked him how the support from the community made him feel.

'It's good man. That's how we live. Brother-in-law, sister, friend neighbour, everybody,' he said.

When we got to the grave, the workmen, who took breaks to sip from cups of soup, chatted loudly.

We stayed for a while, and then were off again. A short old man with liquor on his breath joined us, muttering something about being an ex policeman. He held an unlit cigarette in one hand and a cup in the other. His shoes were muddy and he was the happiest man there. We spent a while with him, laughing at his antics

Johnny Walker

as he frolicked after a full day of helping to dig the grave.

We were on our way back to the van, when we noticed a tall, red-eyed man with dreadlocks running our way. He stopped just short of running me over. 'I man record calypso and reggae,' he said, and broke into song right then and there. I took a step back, slowly inching toward the vehicle. But then the man said, 'I was in Smile Orange. I entertained Charlie Babcock.' A real life celebrity! He gave his name as Johnny Walker. Just then, a car drove by and a man shouted 'Yow, Johnny Walker!'

The lanky man nodded.

'I born and grow in Nonsuch. I have a new single coming. It name 'Time Soft'.' He started singing again. It wasn't half bad. Then again, it may have been the soup.

So that was it. Our visit to 'no such place' was over. Who knew digging a grave could be so much fun?

---

*Note: To the woman I met under the tree: Thanks again, it was really hot, I've never had anything like that before.*

# JOSEPH
# THE OBEAH MAN

**He's perhaps the most famous, feared and at the same time most sought after man in all of Manchester.** Joseph the obeah man has developed quite a following among townsfolk in his quiet community of Walderston and at the same time is well known among diplomats and bureaucrats from more elegant upper St. Andrew addresses.

There have been many tales of Joseph sprouting fire from his fingertips and healing his clients of the most deadly diseases known to man with just a snap of his fingers and the chanting of a few psalms. One woman said she witnessed him levitating one sunny Sunday afternoon.

But despite these stories and the fact that he keeps a crystal ball at his bedside, Joseph isn't your run-of-the-mill obeah man. Sure, he's known around town as a powerful science man, but when photographer Ian Allen and I paid a visit to his small, wooden home in the cool hills of Manchester recently, he was quick to point out that obeah is not all that he does.

'I know about obeah, voodoo, Arabic and Kabbalah. White magic is what it is called. Any problem

you have I can solve it,' he said.

Now, as you perhaps can understand, standing in an obeah man's room was a bit unsettling at first. His house is close to the roadway where he met us. We followed him down a hill before we came across a small, blue, wooden building. He took us to the back of the building and pushed open a wire-framed door. The walls of the room were zinc and wood and there were writings and drawings of symbols and numbers done in red ink all over the walls. There was also something of a price list for the services that Joseph offers. According to the writings, $700 will get you a palm reading or a crystal ball read-up. 'Come in man, you are welcome here,' Joseph said as he led us into a small room. Inside was a bed, a chair, a stool, a table and dozens of photographs pasted on the walls. On a small shelf were many books and a red candle was resting on the table. I noticed a canister, the kind that normally contains insect spray. Only, this was no insect spray. There were drawings of little devils

on the container and it was called something like 'go away evil'.

'This is where I do all the work,' Joseph said.

'Most days you come here you will see a big crowd. People come here from all over the country and even other countries because of all that dem hear about me. Big police and government workers come here to see me,' he proclaimed with a wide grin.

There was a towel hanging on the wall beside a stethoscope and a red rose. He told me to make myself comfortable. I silently contemplated if that was at all possible, especially considering that he was dressed in a long, red robe and his head was wrapped with a red cloth.

I asked Joseph about the services he performs for his clients.

'You name it man. Anything you want done for you I will do it. If you want a visa I have something for that. If you woman leave you I can get her back for you. If you have a court case I will deal with that too,' Joseph pounded his fist into his palm as he spoke and his eyes widened with excitement. He explained that $14,000 will get you a visa to any place in the world you'd like to visit and if the love of your life was silly enough to think she could leave you and go cavorting around town with another, he would get her back for you for a measly $7,000.

# I asked Joseph how he got into the white magic business in the first place.

'Well, when I was 15 somebody try work science on me. Dem put a powder in my hymn book at church and it make my head feel like it was going to tear off! I was sick bad. I decide that I wouldn't want anybody to have that power over me again so I start to read all kind of books. My father was a great science man himself as well so I learn from him and carry on the tradition. I was the only one of his children who carry on the teaching and the work for him,' Joseph said.

He reached behind his bed and pulled out a small, black plastic bag. 'These are some of the herbs I use,' he said.

Joseph showed us bottles containing liquids that he said could cure cancer and mend broken relationships. 'I perform any task the people want. If you sick I have something to heal you. Once you come here and I read you up then I can tell you how to proceed,' he said.

I asked Joseph to tell us about one of the more difficult tasks he's been asked to perform. 'Well you know I will take out duppy and demon out anybody because I am also an exorcist. Well, one day dem tell me that a duppy was in a young boy up the road so I take up my crystal ball and go up there. Well, when I reach I see about 70 people gather around and tell them to move. I look at the boy with the demon and realise that is the duppy of a Indian stillborn baby was in him. Anyway, I chant it out of him and when the people who gather around see what I do dem nearly faint! Dem know dat anybody who conquer a coolie

duppy must powerful!' Joseph said.

Just then, Joseph's cellphone rang and he reached into his pocket and pulled it out. I could hear the voice of the woman on the line asking Joseph for more of the juice he had given her the week before.

When the phone conversation was over Joseph explained that he had to go attend to some clients who had been waiting, so we said our goodbyes and were off. I watched as Joseph slowly disappeared down the hill, closely followed by a slim woman with a cross expression on her face. She was carrying a man's shirt in her hand and was whispering obscenities to herself. I wondered what services she was about to ask Joseph to perform.

# MISSING JAMAICA
# IN LONDON

Standing in line at a small takeout restaurant in Greenwich, London, I noticed a tall, dark man with dreadlocks, standing about 20 feet away. He was the first dreadlocked fellow I had seen since arriving in England. The man was wearing green pants and a black sweater with army style boots and had a stern look on his face.

Beside him was a short, slim, Asian woman who was staring blankly at the menu on the wall in front of her. They were holding hands.

The restaurant was packed and noisy, so everyone was talking loudly. The time had come for me to place my order and, like everyone else, I had to shout it. When I was done, the dreadlocked man walked over to me with a big grin on his face. 'Mi did a wonder if mi know you. But now mi know why mi did feel so. Is because you is a yardy!' he said, chuckling.

He introduced himself as Derrick and mentioned that he was from Old Harbour Bay in St. Catherine. He said he migrated to the United Kingdom more than a decade ago.

'Bwoy, you waan hear seh is just a likkle opportunity reach mi and mi just haffi grab it. I was a fisherman in Old Harbour still, but things wasn't going too well. I had some family up here in the U.K. and they were trying to help me out. When the papers come in, mi really didn't want to leave, but mi did have to think about the money. In Jamaica, all mi a work mi couldn't see anything so even though mi love mi country, mi did have to leave it,' Derrick said. He called over the Asian woman who was standing in line with him earlier and introduced her as his 'dawta'.

She smiled and shook her head quickly and then walked back to where she was before. 'I come up here in 1995. Since that, I go back home about three times, but because of the work mi nuh really able fi go more

than that,' Derrick said. He now works at a car wash in Lewisham where he also lives.

'Is hard work when you come to England still. But you see because you know that when you work, at the end of the day you will see you money, you nuh feel any way. In Jamaica, sometimes mi used to have to wonder why I was working so hard. Couldn't see anything,' he said, shaking his head from side to side.

I asked Derrick how his lifestyle in England differed from when he was living back in Jamaica.

'Bwoy Rasta, a waan tell you dat is a complete difference. Right now, mi really miss home still, but because of the opportunities and the money, I cyaan go back home. Right now, I wish I coulda deh pan a beach wid mi honey and gwaan relax and eat some good food. No place nuh nice like yard, nuh matter what anybody want to say. Jamaica have the nicest life. Is just because a certain struggles why people like me haffi leave. If it wasn't that, then we woulda prefer to stay home. Trust me, living so far from you home get depressing sometime, especially when it cold,' Derrick said.

I asked him what was the most striking difference between life in both countries. 'Well, is just the way people look at you sometimes. In certain place you go, as people start suspect you as a Jamaican, then dem start treat you different. You find that the woman dem will start clutch dem handbag closer under dem arm when you stand up close to dem on di bus or di train. It used to bother me at first because I am no thief, but after a while, you realise that is just so dem stay and you nuh make it bother you,' he said. 'You deh a people country you just have to accept certain things. In some ways, it help mi still because inna Jamaica mi was a ignorant bredda. Yes man! Nobody couldn't talk to me certain way, but when you live a England fi a while, it cool you right down. You cyaan gwaan wid certain things over here, so it force mi fi just easy mi self.'

Derrick said he still has family in Jamaica and sends money to them as often as he can. 'Well, mi know the struggles a yard so whenever mi have a likkle change, mi send it fi mi granny and two cousin dem. Is a good feeling because one time I used to have to depend pon my family a New York fi help me. At least now mi can help out too,' he said. It was here that Derrick seemed to be overcome with thoughts of home. He started asking me how things were before I left.

'Bwoy, people nuh realise how much you miss even the likkle things, when you so far from yuh home. The sun, the people and even di likkle minibus dem dat mi used to hate, now mi miss dem bad bad! Is true man. If mi win some money today, tomorrow mi deh pan a plane. Mi nuh care who waan talk 'bout first world country. Jamaica a mi yard and a deh so a di nicest place fi live. Believe me,' Derrick said with a broad smile.

# JAMAICAN CABBIE
# IN NEW YORK

Now getting around in New York City can be more than a bit tricky for someone who doesn't live there. For Jamaicans, it might be twice as confusing because you can't just flag down a minibus that seems to be going in your general direction. Not that I tried that or anything. But with so many Jamaicans operating taxis and dollar vans all around New York, you're sure to, at the very least, enjoy the ride and have a hearty laugh or two as I found out early one cold Thursday morning when I headed out on a short tour of Brooklyn. I got up early and stepped through the front door of my hotel on Utica Avenue in what I thought were rather warm clothes. Someone mentioned to me that it was 25 degrees outside but I didn't take this warning too seriously.

Five steps through the door however, and I had to make a quick u-turn back up to my room. Ten minutes and four shirts, two jackets, two pairs of socks, a hat, a scarf and pair of gloves later and I was back on the road. Tanya, a voluptuous vixen of a hotel receptionist, told me to head east to the corner of Utica and Eastern Parkway where I'd be able to get a

taxi to wherever I wanted to go. I took her advice and headed off.

About 15 minutes into my walk I started to wonder if I had missed the spot, but then I felt a sudden tap on my shoulder and heard a familiar sound.

'Taxi, bredrin?' His eyes were narrow and he pursed his lips like he was struggling to keep a secret. He wore a large tam and was bulging out of a thick jacket. 'Eh man? You going downtown?' he said in an obviously forced New York accent. When I answered him he seemed to realise that I was Jamaican and his features changed instantly. 'Oh zeen mi bredda. Where you going? Mi cyar park ova deh so,' he said, pointing to a long, black car parked near the sidewalk. I quickly realised that there were several other men standing on the corner whistling to passers-by. 'Taxi madam? Taxi sir?' they said as pedestrians walked by.

'Mi name Desmond, mi will carry you which part you a go,' the man who tapped me on the shoulder said as I walked with him over to his car and hopped inside. It smelled of mangos and there was a small Jamaican flag tied to the headrest. There was a picture of a large, smiling woman in a blue dress taped rather crudely to the dashboard. Peter Tosh's music coming from the giant speakers behind my head added to the, ah ... ambience of the vehicle.

Desmond, it turned out, is from Lacovia in St. Elizabeth and moved to the United States more than 12 years ago. He's about 45 years old now. 'Yes man. Mi haffi come up yah inna di cold fi try make something of myself. It cold and it hard, but you know we Jamaican haffi do what we haffi do,' he said as he drove. Desmond left his wife Patsy and three children back home. 'Bwoy, it was a difficult sinting Pupa, but mi visit dem and ting still. Dem know seh mi haffi a work hard fi support dem, so dem alright,' he said, shaking his head while slowly stroking the picture on the dashboard with his finger. I was getting uncomfortable.

'When mi was in Jamaica mi used to drive truck and ting. But di company I was working wid close down and then hard times reach me. Mi get a little opportunity fi come up here so mi take it and from that, things been going alright. Mi youth dem a go school and mi wife have money fi spend. Is a hard life but it haffi be done,' Desmond smiled as he explained.

I asked him what the hardest part of being away from home was and he grinned. 'Hee Hee. Bredrin a wouldn't know what to tell you. When you live a Jamaica you take everything fi granted. When you leave and come live a different country, den you realise what you have at home. Mi miss di real yard food like breadfruit and di ackee. We get dem ting deh over here, but is not the same. It nuh taste right. Mi miss di Christmas breeze and di pothole dem pan di road. Everything 'bout Jamaica mi miss it,' he said. I was beginning to worry about Desmond getting teary eyed while he drove so I breathed a sigh of relief when he stopped the car. I had reached my destination, so I bid the good fellow goodbye and was off.

I was now in downtown Brooklyn and my plan was to take another taxi from there to get to my final destination in Manhattan. Desmond pointed me in the right direction and told me that I had a good chance of running into another Jamaican driver. 'Is we run up yah so,' he said.

I jumped out of his car and scurried across the road to the spot where he told me I would be able to get another taxi. 'Hey man. How you doing? Can I take you somewhere?' said a man sitting in a grey car. I hopped in and told the driver my destination. 'Oh eem, dat is in Manhattan, right?' he queried and I smiled. Another Jamaican. After I had introduced myself, the elderly man who wore a baseball cap and a pair of glasses smiled. 'I am Trevor, Sar. Good to meet you!' he said in a pleasant tone. Trevor is from St. Ann and has been living in New York for the last 17 years.

'I used to work at the Kingston wharf back in the days as a office clerk. But the manager wasn't dealing with me right so I move up here and start to do some refrigerator repair work. Dat was going on for a while and then I save and buy this car and now is it I use to survive,' he said as he drove.

Trevor moved his wife and three children to New York with him and they all live together in Brooklyn. I asked him if he still visits Jamaica. 'Everytime I can afford it. Is only my mother alone leave over there so I go and look for her alone. I don't go back long time now. I hear dem have big highway now with toll. Hee Hee. Wat a sinting!' he laughed.

I asked Trevor what it was like being a Jamaican taxi driver in New York and he furrowed his brow and went silent for a moment. 'Well, it have it ups and down just like anything. I get hold up two times since I doing this work and the two times is a Jamaican hold me up. But is alright. Dem never hurt me and I continue the work. Is difficult work and the atmosphere not as nice like in Jamaica but because so many Jamaican live in New York I always get to meet them and I like that. Life for Jamaicans up here not so nice and not easy, but you know Jamaican people. Everywhere we go, we do the best we can,' he said.

Miss Matie

# MARVELS OF MOCHO, ST. JAMES

'Clapow!' When I heard the explosion I was about to launch myself head first into a heap of leaves by the side of the road. But luckily, the chuckling woman next to me noticed my bulging eyes and stopped me. 'No young man, it's not a gunshot. Hee Hee. It's the sound bamboo makes when it's burning. Hee Hee.' I got myself together and put on my best I-knew-that expression. 'Remember you're not in Kingston. You're in Mocho,' said the woman, having far too much fun at my expense.

But yes, I was in Mocho. Mocho, St. James. The little known district in the hills of the parish. It's about a mile and a half away from Garlands and down the road from Jointwood.

Photographer Ian Allen and I were standing with a small group of residents in the middle of the road. We had got there only a few minutes earlier. In fact, the minute we arrived, a small crowd descended upon us. But their pleasant smiles and cheerful greetings made us feel welcome.

It was a very bright day and up there in the hills there was a coolness that was extremely relaxing. Other than the intermittent sounds of the burning bamboo exploding in the distance, the place was almost silent. The only sounds were from the birds and every now and again a cow would interject with a hearty moo.

We first met a man wearing a blue shirt and no shoes. He told us to call him Ricky. He was something of an expert on the community and quite a nifty carpenter as well. Other than the few persons who came out to meet us, there didn't seem to be anyone else around. 'Where is everybody?' I asked the community expert. 'Oh, most people gone a bush,' he replied. A couple other people walked up closer and joined the conversation. 'Them out in the field. Other people gone work and some at school. But is not many people live here anyway,' said Miss Chin, whom we later found out was Ricky's wife. 'The best person for you to talk to about the community is Miss Matie,' said Miss Chin, and everyone, even the weird guy who kept whispering to himself, agreed. 'I wonder if she come out pon di veranda yet?' Ricky told us to follow him to Miss Matie's house just down the road. 'She kinda hard a hearing so you haffi shout,' he warned.

Miss Matie's unfinished house was about fifty feet from where we were. We had to go down a few steps to get there. Indeed, she was on the veranda. Miss Matie was a wrinkled, pleasant looking woman wearing a hat and socks with sneakers. 'Howdy Miss Maiti!' shouted Ricky. 'Hello please,' responded the woman, looking off into the distance. Ricky went on to tell Miss Matie that we wanted to know about the community. 'Oh yes man. But you have to bear with me. Mi right eye bad and the other one dark,' she said. The woman said she was 86 years old and lived in Mocho since she was a child. 'I used to chop banana grass. It was hard work but it was good,' she said. She recounted tales of days when the entire community was an estate and belonged to one man. 'Dem days was good. Even now too. Everybody live loving just like first time,' she said, squinting. Miss Maitie said that back in the day most residents worked on the banana plantation. She said that as a young girl she would get excited watching the activities on the plantation.

Now the woman may be getting up in years, but her memory put mine to shame. She went into such intricate details about the different activities on the plantation, that I don't think I'll ever look at a banana the same again.

We soon shouted our goodbyes to the woman and headed off. Ricky told us that there was no piped water in the community. 'The last time I drink chlorinated water was 1988. I was in Montego Bay,' he said, looking off into the distance as if reflecting on the grand experience. 'So where do you get water from now?' I asked. 'Down a hole.' I raised an eyebrow. The man was referring to 'Mas Dickie Pond' which is a tiny spot down the hill where most people get water. With Ricky and Miss Chin leading the way, we started the tiring trek down to the pond. We were walking through knee-high bushes for a few minutes before we finally got to the pond. It was tiny indeed. 'Some people use the water to bathe, but you have to put bleach or Dettol in the water,' said Miss Chin, who was basking in the shade of an overgrown bush. They say the area has quicksand, but some believe that was only a tale to keep the children away from the water. The water was cool and seemed clean enough.

After hanging around for a while, we went back up to the road. Another tedious journey. Up there, we met 'Brother Goodly' who is married to 'Mommy Goodly', who is a teacher at a nearby school. He was decked out in boots, and hat and was wielding a machete. He spoke of his neighbours as if they were all his family members. 'This place is alright man, no problem.' Like Mr. Goodly, many of the residents are proud farmers. There are several acres devoted to yam, corn and potatoes. The roadway and all the homes were spotless. Even the smallest of homes were decorated with beautiful flowers. The view from up there was also spectacular. You could see forever. Or at least until tomorrow. Now about the stigma attached to the name Mocho. Well, these residents seemed not to give a you know what. Everyone we asked about it just chuckled. 'Dem nuh know the place man, dem only a talk,' Ricky said.

When we were leaving, it was like the entire community came to see us off. They all waved and wished us well. Fine people. Now I'm hunting for an excuse to go back.

# SPANISH TOWN:
# A GREAT PLACE TO LIVE

Now I'm a proud Spanish Town resident. Yes, there is such a thing. In my mind, a finer place to live you will not find. All right, stop laughing. The truth is that most persons don't seem to realise that life in the old capital isn't only what they see on television news. So that's why earlier this week, I decided to head right into the heart of Spanish Town, to introduce Jamaica to a side of the old capital they don't often hear about. A place where the faces are friendly, the buildings are beautiful and the atmosphere is welcoming.

However, just in case, on the day I was to undertake this adventure, I got out of bed early, put on my baggiest pair of jeans, ruffled my hair and rehearsed my profanity. Hey, you never know. Eventually, I was ready. Time to hit the road, and hopefully not the pavement.

I commissioned the help of photographer and fellow Spanish Town native, Ricardo Makyn. There's safety in numbers.

We set out to the heart of the old capital just as delivery trucks were making their rounds, dropping off bread and biscuits to different shops across the town. It was a warm and pleasant morning and we got there just in time to watch the vendors set up their stalls.

There was a hint of Christmas breeze, and there was a strong smell of floor polish in the air. Somewhere a radio was playing a slightly distorted version of Bob Marley's 'Exodus'. I was standing on Burke Road, just by the taxi stand, watching an old lady sweep the pavement behind her stall, when suddenly I felt a hand on my shoulder. A raspy voice bellowed: 'Big man, mek you a watch so, you a Kingfish?' I froze; my life flashed before my eyes. I thought I had bought the farm, but when I turned around, I found myself facing the most curious looking character I have ever seen. He was only about five feet tall and his already not so special face was decorated with a scar above his left eye. His asymmetrical head was glistening in the sunlight. His face was of a slightly lighter hue than his neck and arms, and his pants seemed to have been painted on. In my deepest voice, I told him what I was doing and hoped for the best.

To my surprise 'Yes man, mi can tell you 'bout the good thing dem. Long time we want to hear that,' said the unusual looking fellow, who later gave his name as Wayne. Wayne turned out to be a cap and T-shirt vendor who has lived in the Old Capital since he was four. He is now 28. His speech was eloquent.

'Most people think no good come from here. But that is far from true. It is the nicest place to live. Once you work or live in Spanish Town, everybody know you. Anytime you need help you can ask your neighbour and you sure to get it. The best place to be at Christmas time is Spanish Town, pure good vibes.'

A few of Wayne's friends soon joined us and spoke excitedly of playing football in Gordon Pen. They all said it was their favourite pastime. The men also said they enjoyed hanging out together at the different street dances that take place in the town every night. They painted a picture of good food, good music, and beautiful women.

I spent a little while longer with Wayne and his friends and then was off again, having learned something about first impressions. Sitting comfortably in the shade of a supermarket building on Young Street, her feet resting on an empty cardboard box, was 14-year-old Adika Saunders. She said her mother worked in a nearby wholesale shop. 'Of course, Spanish Town nice,' said she. The dimpled young lady explained that she and her mother were originally from the country, but moved to Spanish Town about three years ago. Adika said she loved her new home and would never want to leave.

From there, we went on to the market, located nowhere else but on Market Street. Many of the vendors were still getting their stalls ready for the day. There was a strong fishy smell. Hand-cart men zigzagged through the crowd of early morning shoppers, while portly women sat scraping carrots and cleaning fish.

It was here that we met Norma Morris and Cynthia Ferguson; two smiling middle-aged belles who were quick to explain that Spanish Town was a fine place to live. They said they often go away and leave their goods unattended, without any fear of losing them to thieves. 'The market is always safe. People respect the vendors and we all look out for each other. If my neighbour gone, I will sell for her and she will do the same for me. No worries,' Norma grinned.

We left the market and ventured to the St. Jago High School on Monk Street. We checked in with the security guard and found him a wealth of knowledge of the old capital. He is Barry James and he's been working at the high school for nearly 30 years. It would be difficult to find anyone who knows more about the day-to-day life in the town. 'Yes man, the town is still nice, no matter what you hear. All the students here are like my own and I can tell you that they are all safe. Nobody troubles any of the students and the whole town looks after them. It's like a big family,' he said.

So came the end of a regular day in Spanish Town. Yes, this was the average day in the old capital. A place where strong Jamaican people work hard to make ends meet and where there is always a helping hand when you need it.

# "WOMAN IS MY DOWNFALL!"

The man clutched his Bible tightly in his right hand and used his left index finger to wipe a trickle of sweat from his forehead. His weather-beaten cap cast a shadow over his face and his eyes seemed tired. 'Yes, woman is my downfall!' he shouted. 'Is woman mek mi come from high up and fall to nothing. Dem is pure crosses.'

He was sitting on a large rock near the steps of what's left of his house in the hills of rural St. Catherine. A place called Crawl Pen. The windows of the house were almost all broken and the roof was nothing more than a few pieces of rotting wood and rusty zinc. Now, of course, there are many heartbroken blokes who would say that women have caused them some distress in their lifetime. However, not many of them claim to be able to provide detailed evidence of a woman leading to their demise.

Meet Clement McCalla, known around the Crawl Pen community as Maas Clemmy. Now Mass Clemmy is one bitter fellow and when photographer Norman Grindley and I stopped by to see him recently, he was quick to point out why.

'People ask mi why mi so ignorant. You see how mi place bruck down? Is all because of woman and dem cantankerous ways,' he said. The man pulled aside a piece of sponge that was at the door of the house and then looked me squarely in the eyes. 'You is a young man. You mek sure tek mi advice. Neva you fall in love, for woman will bring you

41

down to nothing,' he said. I looked across at a bucket on the floor used to collect water from the leaking roof and I swallowed hard.

'You remember what Maas Clemmy tell you,' he said. We asked Maas Clemmy to tell us what has now become the well-known story of how he came to this lowly state.

He sighed and then gestured for us to have a seat.

The story goes back to the early 1970s, when Maas Clemmy was a thriving farmer in the community. He claims to have been quite the looker and so was flocked by many adoring females. 'Hee Hee, dem did love me,' he chuckled. But Maas Clemmy was in love with only one woman and he asked her to move in with him. 'Everything was good and tings did a gwaan fi mi. Mi buy mi car and fix up di house,' he said. But then, according to Maas Clemmy, things took a steep dive when after 14 years of waking up to the same face every morning,

he decided to tell his female friend that he wanted to break up with her. 'Mi seh! Is pure crosses from that time!' he said. Maas Clemmy said the woman turned into something of a stalker and wouldn't let him have a moment's peace. 'Everytime mi carry a different lady home with mi, she would come and fling pure stone pan di roof top till di woman frighten and leave,' he said.

Finally, Maas Clemmy could take it no more, so he went up to confront the stone thrower at her house which is just down the road from where he lives. 'Mi ask har what she up to. Di woman go police station go tell dem seh mi threaten fi kill her. Den she go tell everybody in the community seh mi is a obeah man,' he said. Maas Clemmy said that since then, all his friends have turned against

him. With no friends, he had no help when his crops did not come in and so his once thriving farm went south. He soon found himself with no money to insure his car or to repair his house. The car is still parked in his driveway, but completely destroyed from being parked for so long.

'But I should have known. About a month before I run away dat woman, I follow my friend to a reader woman in May Pen. When I find out that is just 50 cent to get a read up, mi decide fi get one myself,' Maas Clemmy said. 'Di reader woman say dat great tribulations will befall mi if mi break up wid mi woman. See it deh now. A pure crosses really deh pan mi,' he said, shrugging his shoulders.

Now, Maas Clemmy spends his days reading his Bible on a giant rock in front of his house. He knows the book so well that he can recite entire chapters off the top of his head. At one point, it seemed like he wouldn't stop.

'Mi read my Bible to kip weh crosses. Is alright though, for I have learned to be alone at this place. People too evil, so mi better off wid me and mi Bible alone,' he said. Maas Clemmy said he thinks that hardships have been at his doorsteps for so many years because he did not sacrifice a pigeon when he was younger. He showed us a Bible passage that he said proves that.

'But God testing me to see what I have inside. Is alright though, as long as mi stay far from woman mi will be quite alright. Woman is where di problem rests!' he said.

# ENCOUNTER IN ALBANY

Now, don't get me wrong, I love a little peace and solitude as much as the next guy. But from past experiences, I thought the people of St. Mary might have been taking things a bit too far. After all, the last time I went there the most exciting thing I could find to occupy my time had to do with a sidewalk that had just been repaved with wet cement, and a clock. Needless to say, I hadn't been back there since.

But anyway, far be it from me to write off an entire parish just because of one uncommonly boring episode. So, along with photographer Norman Grindley, I packed up the car and headed out to the 'banana parish'. Of course, with board games and crossword puzzles in tow, just in case.

The trip to St. Mary from Kingston wasn't that bad. We took the Junction route, passing places like Castleton Gardens and Whitehall. A few - let's say - scantily-clad women, taking their morning dip in a river, waved to us as we passed by. Good times. But after that, well, there was only a vast selection of shrubbery growing on both sides of the road to look at. Nothing fun about that.

We got to St. Mary just before midday. There was a slight drizzle and the sky was grey. We just drove without stopping, through town after town, looking for something interesting. Eventually, after seeing more wild shrubbery than anything else, we decided to stop at a tiny wooden shop on the roadside to chat with somebody, anybody, who could tell us where a good place to visit would be. The second I got out of the car, I heard a man say:

'Hello! Is me you come to?' I turned around. Sitting on a bench made of bamboo was an ageing man with white dreadlocks. He was barefooted and was holding an unlit cigarette in his right hand. 'Ah ... no,' was the reply.

'But is me you must come to. I am the man you want to talk to,' said he. I inched closer to the car. 'Don't run away. Come man. I am Thomas Delarue. I have a story to tell you.' Curiosity made me stay and listen. The dreadlocked storyteller went into an elaborate tale of his days of being a bank robber in the United States. I chuckled. Because he was sitting so close to a bar, I thought he was just in high spirits. He continued. 'But then I get hold in 1973 for robbing a bank in Kingston. I spend 21 years in the Spanish Town prison.' Then he mentioned something about wanting to go back. We sped away, leaving him in a cloud of dust.

We passed a signpost that read 'Welcome to Albany'. We were about to drive right through the community, when I noticed a dark-skinned woman wearing the traditional Muslim headdress, standing at the steps of a large church. Strange mix. Then I noticed another woman in the same kind of headdress, standing behind the counter of a shop. She was completely covered. I could only see her eyes. We decided to stop here for a while. When we got out of the car we noticed two men at a carpenter shop by the side of the road. One was sitting while the other was busy sawing something.

'Hi, I am Marlon Facey, but my Islamic name is Iesa,' said the sitting bloke, extending his hand for a shake. The other man was Tyrone Munroe. 'Tell us a bit about Albany,' I said.

The men told us that the community was made up primarily of persons of the Islamic faith. But, there were also several Christians there as well. 'The main thing about Albany is how peaceful the place is. We all live together peaceful and there is no problem at all,' said Marlon.

'All of us mix up. No matter who is Muslim or Christian. My grandmother is Christian and she don't have a problem with me. All of us help each other, no matter what.'

The people of Albany don't drink alcohol or gamble. In fact, it was the only community we came across where there wasn't a single bar. The Christians only listen to gospel music, and the Muslims, no music at all. The favourite pastime of the young people is football. The teams are evenly mixed with Muslims and Christians. Marlon took us to meet his grandmother. She was sitting on a rocking chair on the veranda of her small house just down the road.

Her name is Hyacinth Bennett and she was born in Albany. She proudly told us that she is a staunch Christian. 'This is the most peaceful community anywhere. It doesn't matter who is Muslim or Christian. When it come down to it, we all are one,' she said. As she spoke, a few chickens were roaming freely in her living room.

'I love Albany. I born here and never leave, so you must know...' CRASH! A loud noise came from inside the house. 'But a wha dis!' she jumped up and ran into the house. 'Shi fowl!' she shouted, and the mischievous fowls scampered away. 'Out of order!' she whispered as she returned.

Ceymore Spencer was sitting with Ms. Bennett on the veranda. 'People can learn from us here. We have other problems, but not with each other. I am Christian, but I respect the Muslims very much. Them kind and helpful,' he said.

We chatted a while with the pair and then left, with Marlon as our guide. We walked through the small community of about 400 residents. Almost directly across the street from a freshly painted church was a mosque. We asked Marlon if he could introduce us to the Muslim woman we had seen when we first got to the community.

'That kind of technical, 'cause you would have to consult her husband and he's not here,' he replied. Marlon did, however, take us to meet 'Sister Amina', who was cutting pieces of coconut in the kitchen of her home. She was also completely covered in a white and orange gown and headdress. We weren't allowed to photograph her, but Sister Amina spoke freely. 'In this one yard, you have my husband who is Muslim, my father who is Adventist and my mother who is Church of God. We all live together, because we are all the same,' she said.

So at the end of the day I had to eat my words. There is nothing dull about St. Mary. Having found so much character and class in only one tiny community, the parish must be a real gem.

# WENTICKO DUPPY!

The second I saw the curtain move in the window of the old duppy house, my knees started to shiver something fierce. Believe me, I was only seconds away from experiencing a massive cardiac arrest right there on the roadway between a stack of logwood and a weird man with a hole in his hat. But luckily, as I grabbed my chest and prepared to meet my maker, I realised that it was only a little girl who had shifted the curtain as she was running by. Whew!

You'll have to forgive me. You see, photographer Ian Allen and I were in Kellits, Clarendon, which is the home of a well-known duppy called 'Wenticko'. Now, as residents tell it, Wenticko is no ordinary duppy. He only comes around once every two or so years, and only around crop time. It being crop time right then, you could understand my fear.

We were standing in front of what is known as the old duppy house. You see, Wenticko makes his presence known by 'going into' the same woman every time he comes around. 'The duppy go inna di woman and do all kinda sinting wid har. Only she him tek set pan and do her all manner of evil,' said one man when we first got to the community. The 'duppy woman's' name is Carrie and, by the tales we heard, has been set upon by Wenticko every couple of years, for more than a decade.

'Him fold her up and put her in a drawer, put her up in a tree top and do all kinda something wid her,' we heard.

It being crop time again, Carrie has gone into hiding. Her neighbours said she was staying with family in St. Ann.

We were standing in front of her house in Kellits where most of the possessions have taken place. There was something really spooky about that place. Then again, that might have just been me. Mavis, a friend, is staying at the duppy house until Carrie gets back.

'Aren't you scared staying in that house?' I asked from a safe distance of about 30 feet from the house.

'No man. Wenticko only come fi di same woman. Is not me him want, so I don't have anything to be scared about,' she said with a that's-obvious-you-idiot expression on her face. The sky was really dark now and I was getting a bit nervous. Well, more nervous.

We asked Mavis and a man in a cowboy hat who had joined us to tell us some of the things Wenticko did to Carrie.

'Dat brute strip her naked, put her up inna tree top and put all gravel inna her food,' Mavis said, a worried look on her face.

'Yes, I saw it with my own eyes,' said the man with the hat. 'Wenticko wrap her hands in front of her and all roll her up the hill. Dat Wenticko, him nuh easy at all,' he continued.

'But why does he only pick on Carrie?' I asked.

'Well, that is a long story. Nuh seh mi seh so, but mi know how it go,' Mavis said. Apparently, one day back in the early 80s, Carrie stumbled upon a man in a very compromising position with a very frightened-looking pig. The story is that Carrie raised an alarm and the pig lover was chased out of the community. In his quest to get revenge on the whistle blower who came between him and his pig, the man went to a 'Madda Woman'. The Madda Woman supposedly set the duppy on Carrie. The duppy was given the name by residents.

Now everyone we spoke with in Kellits has a story to tell about Wenticko. He has been around for so long, that almost everyone who lives in the community has come in contact with him. Church members have visited Carrie's house to try and preach the duppy back to wherever he came from and even Obeah men from near and far have given it a try. But there is only one man in all of Clarendon who can boast that he managed to chase the duppy away. Well, once anyway.

Bredda Boobs is Carrie's uncle and we caught up with him at the local pub.

'Yes man, mi nuh fraid a dat brute,' he said gesticulating wildly.

'I remember it like it was yesterday. Mi just get fed up a di whole thing so mi go down a yard fi di brute. When mi reach inna di house mi see Wenticko have Carrie up inna di ceiling and him call out mi name,' Bredda Boobs was

Bredda Boobs

getting into the spirit now. 'You haffi cuss whole heap a bad word fi get rid a di brute. So mi go in deh go tell him 'bout him what's it not!'

Bredda Boobs, however, said this plan hit a snag.

'Di bugga lick mi dung a ground!' he said, rubbing his temple.

Bredda Boobs said he gathered himself and went to his doctor to get some pills to relieve the pain. When he was feeling better, a light bulb went on in his head. 'Mi seh him is dead and me is alive, so how mi fi come mek him defeat mi? Mi just go ketch a bucket a water and go inna di house go fling it pan him. Heh Heh. You waan see di bugga run out lef Carrie! Heh Heh,' he said, obviously still very proud of himself.

It was now about 6 o'clock, it was getting dark and I started to get a bit antsy. Some smart alec made a joke about the duppy taking a liking to visitors, so I got the you know what out of there, and not a second too soon!

50

# RAINY DAY IN SAV

The sun was already high in the sky by the time Brother Henry arrived at his church. He was late today because his favourite pair of trousers got wet on the clothes line the night before.

'Is pure rain a fall from last week. Mi tell di gyal a yard fi mek sure watch if rain set up and tek up di trousers if anything, but di gyal gone 'bout har business and di trousers soak,' he said, adjusting his wide-brimmed hat. He frowned as he spoke and then made a sucking sound with his mouth.

Brother Henry was one of many people heading out to church in Savanna-la-Mar, Westmoreland, on a recent Sunday morning.

Photographer Norman Grindley and I were standing near to a variety store on Great George Street when we spotted Brother Henry pedalling his bicycle with great fury down the road. He stopped to remove his hat and used ahandkerchief to wipe the sweat from his forehead.

'Every day sun hot and den when night come is pure rain. Mi cyaan chat to you long though, for mi late already. Mi nah get nuh good seat,' he said.

With that, Brother Henry replaced his hat and pedalled off. He caught up with a woman a few feet down the road got off the bike and then the two strolled casually into a nearby church.

We walked along the roadway for a while until we came across an intersection near to what looked like a courthouse. A woman was sitting on the sidewalk behind some bright green breadfruit, some pieces of yam of varying sizes and coconuts. Her eyes were closed and she seemed to be fast asleep. The second we walked over to her, however, she sprung to life.

'How you do? What mi can sell you today?' she said with a raspy voice.

We introduced ourselves and asked her to tell us a bit about Savanna-la-Mar.

'Sav? Yes man. Sav alright. No problem in Sav. Is just di rain waan wash mi out today and di school pickney dem nuh hab nuh manners,' she said.

The woman used the back of her hand to rub her eyes and then seemed more alert.

'Yes, as mi was saying to you. Sav is a likkle place where nobody nuh really faas wid you. If you is selling you likkle thing then nobody not going to molest you wid it. Mi is a old woman now and so mi nuh stay out here all day, but when mi do stay it alright,' the woman said and then turned her attention to a prospective customer.

We said our goodbyes and then walked away. At the end of Great George Street, near to the market, we met a few boys, some of them shirtless, the others shoeless, who were playing with a deflated football.

They were laughing, jumping around and shouting obscenities to each other and seemed to be having a grand time. A grand time, that is, until a heavyset woman whose head was wrapped with a red scarf and who seemed to have been selling in the nearby market spotted them.

'What mi just hear you say, young bwoy?' she shouted.

The boys all stopped in their tracks and turned to face the woman. 'Mi know dat sinting must wrong wid mi hearing for anyhow you really out yah a cuss bad word den a gwine buss you behind today!'

The boys needed no more prompting. They took off immediately, abandoning the football in the street. The woman stood and watched them go, her arms akimbo. When they disappeared, she shook her head and went back inside the market.

Where we were standing, the sea breeze was picking up. The waves actually come right up to the market and close to the road, making a beautiful scene.

The clouds started to get ominous and a few drops of rain started to fall. This hastened activity on Great George Street quite dramatically. People started running about in haste, shouting in many different ways that the rain was about to fall.

The woman who was earlier sitting lazily beside her coconuts and breadfruit, grabbed them up in a hurry, threw them in a box, put the box on her head and scampered off with the speed and agility of a 20-year-old. After that, the streets emptied in a hurry and the rain came with a fury, bringing a sudden end to another lively day in 'Sav'.

# TOMBSTONE MYSTERY!

Now as far as I'm concerned, what happens between a man and his donkey in private is his own business. But I must admit that I was a tad curious when I heard that so strong was the love between the man and his beast, that the two were buried together!

Eerie, I know. But the only way to find out more about this creepy story was to head down to the spot where the bodies of the man and his beloved steed are rumored to be buried.

As the story was told to me, the couple lived a long and happy life together in a lowly hut in the bushes of St. Elizabeth back in the 1940s. Yes, theirs was apparently a close bond that led the old farmer to request that his donkey be buried with him when he died. That's all I could find out, so I commissioned the help of photographer Ian Allen and headed off to a place called Tombstone, St. Elizabeth, where it is said the remains rest.

Now it was easy to tell why the place is called Tombstone. Two large concrete tombs which, it is said, house the remains of the donkey-loving man and the apple of his eye are the most noticeable things in the entire square. There is a gas station behind the tombs and a few small shops across the road. The tombs are right beside the road with cars whizzing by all day.

We hopped out of the car and walked over to a small shop where a woman was enjoying an afternoon snooze behind the counter. I cleared my throat but she didn't move. I poked her with my finger but she didn't budge. I was about to count my losses and walk away when a man wearing a torn T-shirt walked up to the counter. 'Iris! Serve here!' he shouted. This jolted the woman out of her peaceful slumber. She was not amused. 'Ah wah do you? Mek you so cantankerous? You nuh see mi a sleep?' she retorted.

The man requested a bottle of oil and when the exchange of money for bottle was made, he was off. 'Afta mi and you nuh quabs!' Iris whispered under her breath when he was gone.

Perhaps against better judgement I decided to go ahead and ask the miserable woman about the tombstones. To my surprise, it went quite smoothly. 'Oh. Well nobody know is who really bury there still. People say all kinda things still. Some say is a man and him donkey, other people say is a soldier and all kinda thing,' she said.

'Some people say is a evil woman from inna olden times dat bury there and the other grave is her fandangle dem weh she use to work her evil,' she said.

Two men walked up to us and joined in the conversation. They said they operated the small shop right across the road from the tombs. 'Dem say is a British soldier and him horse bury there. And some writing deh pan it. But nothing nuh go so!' said the shorter of the two men. He was a stumpy little man with bushy eyebrows. The other man was tall and lanky.

'Is two man was having a drink one day long ago in a bar over there,' the short man pointed

across the road. 'The two of them get into argument over woman business and then them decide fi have a duel,' he said, using his fingers to imitate a gun.

'But in them days you never have nuh gun,' he said, calling into question his finger imitation.

'Them use sword and chop up one another and is the two of them bury there 'till this day,' he said with a look of satisfaction on his face.

The tall man had a look of disgust on his face. 'You is a fool! Is the British soldier bury over there with him horse! Everybody know that,' he quipped. As he put it, many people have seen the ghost of the soldier and his horse late at night. 'Mi know people who see the duppy dem. So mi know seh is true,' he said.

We decided to walk over to the tombstones to see if there were any inscriptions on them. Indeed there were, but they had faded with time and were hard to read. I did manage to decipher part of the inscription on one of the tombs though, which explained that it was indeed the burial spot for a British soldier called Thomas Spence who died in the 1700s. The other tomb had no inscription.

We met Veronica Lawrence, a heavyset woman who was wearing a long blue dress and a pair of glasses. She explained that even though the inscriptions say that the tomb houses the soldier's remains, not many people in the community buy that story.

'People have their own story and not many people believe that it's the soldier,' she said.

We soon proved the woman's statement.

As we walked around and spoke with some longtime residents of the area, we realised that we didn't get the same explanation from any two persons. Everyone had a different story.

'Is Mary Lee bury there,' one woman said. When we asked her who Mary Lee was, she stuttered. 'I don't know, I only hear that is a woman name Mary Lee bury there,' she answered finally.

We managed to find out that there is a popular fable that a woman named Mary Lee was riding on a horse with her male friend. The story is that she was feeling a bit, well, gassy and dropped dead at the very spot where the tombs are now.

Brother Bean, who was standing a few feet from the concrete structures, told us that he thought the tombs were cursed. 'If you ever know how much car crash inna dem ting deh, and all now dem can't mash up,' he said. 'Mi see about hundred car and truck inna my lifetime crash inna dem and and dem still there. Mi nah waste no time a gues who inna dem, for it ago deh 'bout longer than me and you!'

# SANDY BAY MYSTERY HOUSE

There's a spooky old house on a lonely corner in Sandy Bay, Clarendon, where mystery and tales of horror are the order of the day. Stories of ritual sacrifices and animal beheadings leave many with sweaty palms and sleepless nights. There's even one famous fable of an unfortunate preacher who paid a visit to the house to find out exactly what was going on there. As the story goes, he went in, but never came back out. There are many who dare not tempt fate and walk on the opposite side of the road when going by the house. Now none of these stories have ever been confirmed, so to get to the bottom of the mystery, photographer

Norman Grindley and I said goodbye to our families, whispered a prayer and headed off to the enigmatic edifice.

As luck would have it, it was an overcast, wet and dreary day. This didn't do much to calm my fears, but I put on a brave face as we approached Sandy Bay. We got wind of exactly where the house was, so as we got closer, my stomach started to churn. We heard that in the yard, there were about 15 large flags, all of different colours and as we turned a corner after crossing a train line, there it was.

The very sight of the place gave me the heebie jeebies. Sure enough, the flags, which were attached to large bamboo poles, were fluttering menacingly in the wind. Large trees and other shrubbery blocked our view of the house. We could only get a glimpse of the building in the background. It was blue and seemed rather large. To be safe, we drove by slowly and went down the road without stopping. Instead, we went about a half mile away and stopped at a small shop to find out more about the place.

We met Suzette, who works at the shop, and asked her to tell us what she knew of the strange place. 'Mi hear all kinda sinting. Dem seh a obeah woman live over there. Other people say is a poco church. Mi nuh know a wah over there massa, but mi nah go over there fi ask,' the woman said with a vigorous shake of the head. 'You know dem poco church people deal inna all sort a something. If mi go over there dem probably go wuk science pon mi!'

Now these were by no means reassuring words, but the time had come to bite the bullet and put the mystery to rest.

We hopped in the van and went cautiously back up to the house. This time the gate was open so we parked outside and walked slowly up to the house.

The sound the flags were making as they fluttered made me even more uncomfortable. I realised that there were crosses printed on them. There were writings on the ground, but none of it made any sense to me. There was a white container filled with water on a table under a tree. About a dozen drinking glasses were placed around the yard. They too were filled with water.

'Er ... Ah hello?' my voice had a nervous squeak to it as I called. A middle-aged woman wearing a hat poked her head through a window. She soon disappeared. I got nervous and was ready to leave, but stopped in my tracks as I saw the woman coming towards us. She didn't look like an obeah woman to me. 'Hello,' she said rather bluntly. She wasn't smiling and she looked at us quite quizzically. As a trickle of sweat ran down my forehead, I explained to her the tales we had heard of the place and told her we had come to find out the truth. I was sure this would have upset her, so I braced myself to be zapped into a frog. To my surprise, the woman started to chuckle hysterically.

'Hee hee. That is what people always believe. Some say is an obeah woman live over here and that we even take money to have people killed.

Hee Hee. Don't worry, none of it is true,' she said, sensing my unease. I was much relieved by this and started to ask more questions.

## As it turns out, the building is the home of the 'Resurrected Church of God, Mount Zion', which is a Revival church. 'It is different from a poco church. We worship the same way, but it's different,' the woman explained.

'So why all the mix up?' I asked. 'Well many people think

my mother is an obeah woman because of her powers,' said she. My discomfort returned. 'But she only uses her powers to serve the Lord. She heals people, she doesn't hurt them. She gets visions from God and uses them to help other people,' the woman, who gave her name as Sister Smith, explained.

'Everybody calls my mother 'Madda'. She is the pastor for the church. She is powerful and can heal people. In fact, if she wasn't anointed by God, her powers could do great evil and bring tribulations upon the earth. But she is a good

woman,' Sister Smith said.

We asked if we could meet Madda. Sister Smith looked us up and down as if assessing our worth. 'She might not talk to you but I'll ask her. If her spirit don't tek to you, she not going to talk to you,' she said and went inside to Madda.

Soon the elderly woman appeared. Surprisingly, she had a pleasant face and was smiling. 'How do you do?' she asked.

Madda explained that she knew of the stories people told of her.

'But I am here doing the Lord's work. People even afraid to walk near here. But there are those who also think we work obeah and come here for all manner of evil. Some big society people come and asking for demonic assistance. But I not into that,' she said.

'Just last week a man knock on the gate and when I answer, him

seh, "You kill people?" When I seh no, him just walk off,' Madda chuckled as she recalled. 'I get visions about people who I don't even know and I travel across the country to help them. It's what I do. But we Revivalists are peculiar you know. If I wasn't one, I would be scared too. So I don't blame people,' Madda explained.

I asked her what was the significance of the flags and the containers filled with water. 'Water is our calling. It's purity. The flags represent different nations. You wouldn't understand unless you're a Revivalist.' She took us into the church. There was a small pool of water and a table with bottles of cream soda, dried coconuts and grapefruits. A single red candle was placed at the entrance. There were some plants near the water and I asked what they were. 'That's leaf of life. We use it in healing. The cream

soda and coconuts use with calanga water for the same thing. We break them to get rid of evil spirits. But you have to believe or it not going to work for you,' she said. Madda took us to the prayer room where there was another pool and even more bushes. There were even more soda bottles placed neatly in a row. 'This is where the healing take place. God is in this room, so it's a powerful place. Is because people don't know, that's why them tell so much lies on us,' she said.

Soon we went back outside. Madda was pensive as she spoke. 'People need to know that is not just about cream soda and calanga water. We are Christian soldiers, so there's no need to fear us. Anybody who want evil works to be done, go somewhere else. We are friendly people and only want to help.'

# HEALING POWERS OF SALT RIVER

Let's face it, there's nothing particularly inviting about the name Salt River. I mean in a country which has so many rivers with more romantic monikers like the tantalising Rio Minho and the alluring Rio Cobre, Salt River is a bit of a drag.

For most persons, Salt River is the kind of place that they only drive pass on the way to another destination. I mean, really, just driving by the spot, there doesn't seem to be any reason to stop. But the memorable caresses of a buck-tooth 200-pound female with whom I had something of a fling in high school, made me realise that you should never judge a book by its cover. Good old Lavern.

That's why earlier this week, photographer Ian Allen and I set off to Salt River to get to the meat of the matter.

Now the journey to Salt River, after you pass Old Harbour, is something of a roller coaster ride that seems to go on for miles. I mean miles.

But after travelling along the bushy, pothole-filled road for a while, we finally came upon the first sign of life. The first living thing we had seen in quite a while. We saw something moving behind a rusting sign that read something about 'Welcome' and 'River.' Screech! When the dust cleared we found ourselves face to face with a sorry-looking group of donkeys. They stared at us for a while, and call me crazy, but I swear one of the brutes gave me a threatening look. I don't take chances with four legged beasts of any sort, so we jumped back into the car and sped off.

Just down the road we noticed a group of persons sitting at what looked like a shop. We went over to meet them.

'Hail! Hail!' the group said in unison before we could even get out a word. 'Sit down, man, what you want to know?' asked a bespectacled man with dreadlocks. He was sipping from a plastic cup and puffing on a cigarette.

'Tell us about Salt River,' I said.

An elderly bloke wearing a weather-beaten hat spoke up. 'The place alright, man. Back in the day you used to have ships coming here. That don't happen anymore so most people around here turn to fishing,' he said to nods of agreement from his companions.

There are about a thousand persons living in the Salt River community, most of whom are fisherfolk. Including, by the way, a female shopkeeper who was quite eager to show us her, ah … gear.

The area was once a bustling little port, where ships full of all kinds of goods would dock. 'It did exciting dem time deh. When me

ARE YOU SICK AND TROUBLE
COME SEE THE SPIRITUAL PHYSIC
THE LORD HAS RISEN US UP TODAY WIT
GREAT HEALING AND DELIVERANCE -
THERE IS CURE FOR CANCER-SUGAR/DIAB
GAUL STONE - GROWTH & NERVOUS CONDIT
FOR GREAT HEALING & DELIVERANCE CONTACT-BRO. LL
27 SEWELL CRESCENT. TEL. 337-9833 MAY
COMING FROM THE ORDER OF KING SOLO

and niceness,' he said, with a lisp.

'Mi seh bredrin. You see all di one weh name Pigeon Island? It well lookable you know mi bredda! Better than Negril!' He really was getting excited now. Ezekel said Pigeon Island was about nine miles away from shore. 'When mi boat a work, mi carry people go out deh fi enjoy themself,' he said.

He described the beaches in the Salt River community and on the islands surrounding the area with such excitement and detail that he could just as well have been describing his girlfriend.

Chakka, a Rastafarian with what seemed like a permanent expression of anger on his face, joined in. 'We have a lot of things here fi see. Mocho rabbit and crocodile like nothing!' He tried to explain what a Mocho rabbit

was, but I ended up feeling more confused than ever.

'Crocodile?' I asked with obvious trepidation. 'Hee hee, har har,' was the reply from the experienced fishermen. I was red in the face. 'I mean, you know, I ... ah ...' I tried to cover things up, but alas it was too late. 'Dem won't molest you unless you molest dem. Dem more run from you,' said Chakka. 'Although dem a nyam off di dog and di goat dem. I mean dem can gwaan with the dog dem. Although dem bark after people still. But dem nuh fi mess wid di goat dem!'

I had heard stories of persons travelling from far and wide to Salt River, solely for what is believed to be the river's healing capabilities. It is said that the water can cure diabetes, cancer and anything else you throw its way. I asked about this.

'Yes! It's true!' Everyone had a story. Ezekel said people travel from all over the world to a pond down the road from where we were to heal themselves of all kinds of sicknesses. 'Mi see a man

did likkle we used to run up and down and look pan di ship dem,' said the man with the hat, who by the way kept looking at my shoes. I don't question these things.

Ezekel Stanford, who wore a red tam and a curious looking pair of shorts, told us that most people don't realise just how much Salt River has to offer. 'We have 14 islands 'round here man. Pure fun that get strokes and couldn't move get heal! Mi see that myself!' he said.

Ezekel said you could see the minerals in the water. 'You know when you a drink rum and water? You can see the rum different from the water. Is same way you see the minerals and water different.' He actually went on for a while about the rum and water with a longing look in his eyes, but I didn't wait around for him to snap back to reality.

We walked down to the pond and found a few people splashing around and having a grand time. A few shops were open, where cooks were busy at work preparing fish, festivals and other delights. There was a large tree nearby, with several carvings. This, coupled with the scantily clad women splashing around in the pool, made an enticing scene. I stayed and watched a while.

But alas, it was getting late, and the women may have been getting a bit nervous, so we decided to leave and head back to Kingston with knowledge of one more hot spot on this beautiful island we call home.

# RUMBLE IN ST. THOMAS

In a tiny shoemaker's shop on a lonely street in rural St. Thomas, there's an argument raging between a stubborn old shoemaker called Clifton Rumble and an even more headstrong, churchgoing woman called Sister Gatty.

It was early afternoon when Sister Gatty, a slim, bespectacled woman wearing a hat, strolled into Maas Rumble's tiny wooden shop with a black plastic bag in her hand and greeted the gangly man.

He was fast asleep on a chair at the time.

'Mawning,' she shouted, using the bag in her hand to hit the man's foot, giving him a good jolt. 'Ahhh,' was Maas Rumble's response as he opened his eyes. 'You cyaan seh mawning? You a big man. You fi ha mannas!' Sister Gatty's nostrils seemed to flare as she shouted. 'Evey day a di same sinting. Why you won't learn?' Maas Rumble was by now, noticeably peeved.

'Anyway, is mi old boot mi carry fi you patch up,' Sister Gatty said, reaching into her plastic bag and taking out a pair of white sneakers.

'All right, just siddung mek mi do it,' Maas Rumble mumbled as he reached for a small can containing a yellow paste.

It was then that photographer Norman Grindley and I introduced ourselves to the pair. 'Well, I am the original one and only shoemaker in town. But mi soon lef it and go tend to mi pig dem. Mi cyaan badda wid di baddaration,' were Maas Rumble's first words to us.

'You hear di man dem ask you 'bout you and you pig dem?' Sister Gatty interjected.

'Woman kirout!' Maas Rumble shouted and then turned back to us. 'Shoemaker work get really slow right now. It nuh mek nuh sense again. So mi soon decide fi go raise two goat and two hog and take a hard life easy,' he said.

We asked Maas Rumble to tell us a bit more about himself.

'Well, I born and grow right here in Seaforth. I am really a butcher, but things slow up now. Mi fix lantern too. Mi have 21 pickney, nine slut and 12 bull. Dem big now and move out. So is me one deh here now a gwaan banga banga,' he said. Sister Gatty sent a disgusted look his way.

'Me is a man love drink mi white rum. Rum bar a di greatest college. It teach you more than any school and any church,' said the

66

man. It was then that all hell broke loose.

'You a sin yuhself! You a call down judgement pan yuhself!' Sister Gatty pointed her finger in the air as she shouted. She wiggled in her chair as if she had suddenly been taken over by an outside force. 'There will be weeping and moaning. Nuh sin yuhself so!' But Maas Rumble would have none of it.

'Mi seh rum bar better than any church. You learn more 'bout God inna rum bar,' he said. 'God is inna yuh heart. Him nuh inna nuh building.'

This sent Sister Gatty up the roof. 'But you need place fi assemble. What kinda foolishness you chatting? Mi a go church fi nearly 30 years and nobody cyaan tell mi seh mi nuh fi go. Look yah, just mek haste fix mi boot mek mi gallang!' she shouted back at him.

Maas Rumble shook his head and then turned to me. He explained that as a child, he was a frequent churchgoer, until one rainy Sunday afternoon when he was 12 years old, his pastor

approached him after services. 'Him gimmi a note and ask mi fi deliver it to Miss Cherry. Him seh mi should not tell anybody about it and mi should not read it. Anyway, I was a young boy and very curious, so I take the note and go one side to read it. I remember what that note say until this day,' Maas Rumble gazed at the sky as if lost in memory.

According to the shoemaker, the note said 'I don't have much time. I cannot let my wife find out, but leave the back door open and I will see you in a little while.'

Maas Rumble chuckled. 'From mi read dat, mi seh mi not going back inna nuh more church.'

Sister Gatty was livid. 'Stop tell di man dem lie and make haste wid mi shoes. Smaddy down a yard a wait pan mi!' she said.

The woman grabbed the shoe from Maas Rumble's hands and in no time was off down the road. The last thing I heard her mumble

was something about fire and weeping. 'Nuh pay har nuh mind. Is mi friend,' Maas Rumble said when the woman was well down the road. Always the talker, the shoemaker started to tell us more about his tiny shop. It was made of wood and sheets of zinc that were brown with rust. 'I been here fi so much years. This place get lick by di 51 storm, Gilbert and Ivan and it never damage yet. Is it mek mi survive fi so many years. When I was younger I used to fix lantern alone. Then I was a butcher and then mi leave dat fi go drive taxi. Now mi a fix shoes and lantern and soon start raise back some more pig,' he said.

There were several lanterns hanging in the small shop. I asked Maas Rumble if they were all given to him to be fixed. 'Some of them is mine. I don't believe inna electric light. No sah. That will blind you. I only use lantern. Di electric light only dazzle yuh eye dem,' he said.

We asked him to tell us how he found life in Seaforth. 'Well, things quiet here for di most part. But when I was a bwoy it was more better. Mi used to ride mi donkey go anywhere at anytime. Dem was di days,' he said, smiling.

Just then, an elderly man rode up on a bicycle. He was clutching a small lantern in his hand. 'Maas Rumble!' he shouted. With another customer turning up, we decided to bid Maas Rumble farewell. 'All right, we will link up one day and drink two white rum,' he shouted after us with a chuckle.

# EASY, BREEZY BANANA GROUND

Now it seems that Ms. Chunie has come down with a terrible case of the sniffles, which her neighbours in the small community of Banana Ground in Manchester believe resulted from her refusal to 'come off a di veranda' before nightfall. Now Ms. Chunie is one tough woman who for some reason, doesn't trust doctors, so she sent her granddaughter to Ms. Margaret's shop to fetch her some molasses. She'll fix the problem herself.

Now this is where the story picks up. Photographer Norman Grindley and I were standing in Ms. Margaret's shop when Ms. Chunie's granddaughter walked in.

'Ms. Margaret! Ms. Chunie say if you can send one bottle a molasses,' the girl muttered, her head barely making it to the top of the counter. She couldn't have been more than four years old, and was clutching a black plastic bag in one hand and a tightly folded $50 bill in the other.

Ms. Margaret took a bottle off the shelf and handed it to the little girl in exchange for the money. The bottle was labelled white rum, but contained a dark brown liquid. 'Tell Ms. Chunie never mind, dis will fix it,' Ms. Margaret said to the little girl and the youngster scampered off.

Now with nobody else in the shop, we got to know Ms. Margaret a bit better. You see, we were in Banana Ground for only a few minutes and nearly everyone we met, told us that we should go introduce ourselves to Ms. Margaret.

So there we were, in a rickety old shop in a small community in the hills of Manchester with the most famous woman in the area. Ms. Margaret has been running the small shop since 1953 and is considered the community expert. We asked her to tell us about Banana Ground.

'Well it not very different from what it was even when I just started this shop,' the woman said. As she spoke, some school boys walked into the shop. **'The place still quiet and cool. It's very breezy. That's why we don't plant things like banana up here.'** Now that made my head spin. 'What?! They don't grow bananas in Banana Ground?' I asked.

'Have me excuse?' Ms. Margaret said. She doesn't hear as well as she used to. I repeated my question. 'Oh well, back in the once upon a time, dem used to was plant plenty banana up here, but it too breezy man. It would mash up di tree dem,' she said, giving the school boys who were playing among

themselves and getting a bit loud, an angry look. The look brought the boys to immediate silence.

A little girl walked in and without hesitation shouted, 'Ms. Margaret, gimme one dutty gyal soap please!'

'Pickney kibba you mouth! When you see big people a talk you fi cry excuse! What wrong with you? Tell di gentleman dem good morning! You a jing bang?' Ms. Margaret was livid and her glasses almost fell off her face.

The girl now had a dejected look on her face and started staring at her shoes. 'Good morning,' she whispered, bending her right knee slightly. 'Now go and stand up one side and wait till we done,' Ms. Margaret said. The girl dragged her feet to the corner of the shop and stood there pouting.

There was a strong smell of kerosene in the shop. I realised that a large cylinder that was at the entrance to the shop, was filled with kerosene. That's the only source of the product in all of Banana Ground.

Ms. Margaret went on like nothing had happened. 'Yes, and here is very quiet. You open your door and leave it. Get up and walk outside anytime and nothing is wrong. You in peace up here,' she said. The woman said she has spent most of her life in the small farming community, which is home to only a few hundred persons. She even went to the small school just down the road from the shop.

We decided to visit the school, so we bid the woman farewell. But before we did, we told her we wanted to snap a picture of her. 'Oh yes man, I'm coming,' Ms. Margaret said and retreated into a back room. What was going on? After about 15 minutes the woman reappeared, dolled up in a completely different outfit, a new hat and without her glasses. The woman smelt of roses. We snapped the pictures and were off. 'Tek care now and God bless,' Ms. Margaret sent us off.

We went over to the Garlogie Primary School and met up with a group of boys playing cricket in the road. They used pieces of wood as bats and a tennis ball and were having a great time. 'Mister, you is from Merica?' said one lad, shading his eyes from the sunlight. 'You a idiot? You nuh see a car dem come inna? Dat look like plane?' another boy interjected.

We spent some time with the group, but soon it was time to leave. As we got into the van and drove off, a long line of children started running behind the vehicle, waving goodbye. Quite a friendly bunch of people.

# AN AUDIENCE WITH THE DUMPLING EMPRESS

I love me a good dumpling. It's true. To me, nothing beats a plump, well-designed, succulent fried dumpling, with just a smidgen of 'salting'. I can taste it now. From that first whiff you get when it is fresh off the fire, to that heavenly moment when your lips and tongue slowly caress the contours of the tantalizing treat. Yummy.

Now I'm sure you'll all agree that there's no dumpling like a homemade dumpling.

There's just something about the way they're prepared. But I recently heard of an unassuming middle-aged woman who runs a shop in the heart of Christiana, who might just leave you thinking differently. She gives her name as simply 'Miss Norma', but the satisfied people of her hometown have crowned her the 'Dumpling Empress of Christiana'.

This sounded like my kind of woman. So last week, photographer and fellow dumpling connoisseur Norman Grindley and I, loaded up the van and sped off to meet this dumpling-making belle.

We got to Main Street, Christiana, just about midday and found the town alive and kicking. That normally cool Manchester atmosphere took on a particularly seasonal feel. The sun was out in full force and there wasn't a cloud in sight.

After driving in circles for a while, we found a parking space just in front of a bar, across from the taxi park. Gospel music was blaring from a small radio at the entrance to the park.

We got out of the van and looked up. A sign above an open doorway read 'Don Jones Bar'. This was the place. Time to meet the Dumpling Empress.

So into the spacious bar we went. It was rather cozy. There were cushioned seats all around and a nicely decorated dining table. A few elderly men sat together on wooden bar stools drinking and swearing in a most alarming way. But their swearing just as soon broke out into laughter, of the toothless kind.

But there was nobody who fit the description of the Dumpling Empress. My belly growled. Then suddenly a head poked up from behind a counter.

She was about 55 years old. A round woman with golden brown skin. Something familiar here. Anyway, this was the Dumpling Empress, we were sure.

There was a container on the counter full of large, round, fried dumplings and chunks of saltfish as big as a fist.

We questioned the woman. 'Yes man, people love my dumplings. Nobody can test my dumplings,' said she with a wide, bright smile.

So what makes her dumplings so special?

'Mine are soft and nice. It's all in the oil. People don't understand the oil. You have to know how hot to make it and when to take it out.' She really started to get excited now. I was a bit taken aback.

It was just after midday and while the woman said these words, two hungry looking patrons came into the shop to buy 'some a di dumpling dem.' One of the customers, a bespectacled, slender female, started smiling the second Miss Norma handed her a brown paper bag with the goodies. People travel from all over to buy these dumplings. Miss Norma said many people have told her that they heard about her cooking prowess from friends.

**The famous dumpling maker said that on a good day, she can breeze through 12 pounds of flour, easily. In a single day!**

At $10 a pop, it seems Miss Norma is on her way to building quite the dumpling empire. 'Just the other day one woman come in and buy 20 dumplings one time. I run out and the woman just sit and wait,' she chuckled.

Now remember, Miss Norma is about 55 years old, and she's working in a bar.

'That is strange, but it's alright. The crowd this old woman draw, no young girl can test!' she gleamed.

76

But she is a strict bartender. If you're a student, don't even think about trying to get a drink to buy in Miss Norma's bar. 'Oh no. None of that. They cannot come in here with that.' But Miss Norma's winning personality has gained her the respect of the townspeople. Everyone who came in while we were there, addressed her as 'Miss Norma' and were sure to say please when asking for something from behind the bar. No matter how inebriated they seemed. We found it hard to part company with this pleasant woman, but we sure will never forget her and her dumpling-making ways.

So back into the streets we went. You know what surprised me about the people from that part of Christiana? They were already well into their Christmas festivities in November. I mean well into it.

We walked down a narrow street that had been transformed into a market. It being mid-November, we asked the vendors if they planned to start selling sorrel anytime soon. The response was mixed with laughter: 'That done

long time, you late!' Townspeople, we were told, had shopped months ago and by now, were already drowning in sorrel and fruit cake.

But that doesn't mean that the Christmas excitement was over. Far from it. People we talked to, said Grand Market in Christiana is unlike any celebration anywhere else. The countdown to that festive day has already started.

While we were in the market, I heard a loud rumble and a dejected moo. That's right, a moo. Not a combination of sounds you hear everyday. I turned around and saw that a large blue and white

truck with about three cows in the back, was slowly making its way through the crowd. Not exactly something you see on Knutsford Boulevard in St. Andrew on any given Friday.

The cows were on their way to meet their maker via a nearby butcher shop. Poor things. Well, at least we know there will be no meat shortage this Christmas.

So, having met a world-renowned dumpling expert and witnessed the final pre-slaughter expedition of a few noble cows, we had quite a full day. Time to head back to Kingston and a life of mediocre dumplings.

# THE DEVIL'S WATCHGLASS

The woman said that the giant crater was caused by some sort of demonic force. Her forehead crinkled as she frowned and she looked at me with eyes that said, 'Why would anyone want to go there?'

Now this didn't sit well with me, especially standing there on a dirt road in the middle of nowhere. The sun was going down and it transformed the sky into a haunting red. It was like the sky was bleeding. A drop of rain fell on my nose. I started to regret this trip.

The giant crater that the woman was talking about is known as God's Well and it's at the border of Manchester and Clarendon. It's been around for as long as anyone can remember and from what we heard, stories about the origins of the giant sinkhole range from academic to just plain silly.

Residents of communities nearby say that divers from around the world have visited the giant hole and no matter how hard they tried, they have never been able to reach the bottom of it.

'A di devil watchglass! Him sit down pan him chair an look out pan we!' said one frightened looking old man when we asked him about the hole. 'Do, nuh badda go deh so!' A chilling warning indeed.

But with all these tales circulating about the enigmatic crater, I just had to see it for myself. So, I called on photographer Norman Grindley and we headed off to find the 'devil's watchglass'.

When we got to Clarendon, we weren't exactly sure where to go next. So we stopped in a community called Milk River to ask for directions. A short, fair-skinned woman was sitting behind the counter at a grocery shop. We asked her about God's Well. A quizzical look came to her face and she started to explain that the hole was cursed and that nobody should go there alone. 'A white man and his wife went there and never came back out alive. Take my advice and stay far from that place!' she whispered.

I won't lie. This did make my knees wobble a bit, but press on we did. The woman pointed us in the general direction of God's Well and bid us goodbye. Somehow it seemed that she thought we would never return.

We were on a completely deserted road with nothing but

bushes on either side. No sign of life. Soon enough though, we came across three men walking along the road. They wore water boots and carried machetes.

We stopped to ask directions.

'God Well? A deh so you a go? It inna one bush you know!' said the shortest of the three. His front teeth were missing and he smelled of rum. He wobbled a bit as he approached my window. One of the other men, a husky fellow wearing a pair of very dark sunglasses, grabbed the spirited fellow by the shirt collar and pulled him back. 'It deh up di road! Just go up likkle and go round likkle bit and you see one big tree beside one next tree. You can't miss it,' he said.

The third man, who also smelled of rum, chimed in. 'It inna di bush! Don't go there! You want mi fi carry you?' He leaned in and poked his head through the window. We sped off and left him in a cloud of dust.

A bit further down the road we came across a man riding a bicycle.

Praying for better luck, we asked him about God's Well. He looked us up and down and then said we had just passed it.

'You not going to find it by yourself. Follow me and I will show you,' he said and turned his bicycle around.

He rode about a quarter mile back in the direction he was coming from and signaled for us to park by the side of the road.

The man walked over to us and stuck out his hand. He gave his name as 'the deacon'. I took a step back.

'We have to walk about five minutes that way,' he said, pointing into the bushes. I could hardly figure out how we were going to make it. There didn't even seem to be a track to follow. But before I could say anything, the deacon was off.

'Watch di macca tree! If dat ketch you, you goose cook!' the deacon shouted. He was now about a hundred yards ahead of us. We walked over fallen trees and rocks and passed over a few dead birds before we finally got to the giant crater.

## 'Mind you drop over inna it!' the deacon shouted.

The hole was huge and went hundreds of feet right down. Stagnant, murky water was settled at the bottom of it and the remains of a few dead animals floated on top. The spot looked like a huge meteor had crashed right through the earth. It was like a bad dream.

'Bwoy mi nuh like it you know,' the deacon said. 'Mi nuh like come here but sometime some tourist come here and ask mi fi show dem. Mi just carry dem and run lef dem. Mi nuh inna it massa.' The deacon had a worried look on his face.

He said that a few years ago, a married couple from the United States visited the spot. Being adventure lovers, they decided to dive into the spooky looking water to see if they could make it to the bottom of the hole. The deacon said this was something that many people have done, yet no one has ever been able to find the end of the crater.

'The woman drown inna one cave below di water and the husband almost dead too. Dem say di place a crosses so mi always tell people nuh fi try go too close,' said the deacon. There was a small crocodile wading through the water. We asked the deacon about it.

'Yes man, is long time him deh yah. Mi know him 'bout five years now and him nah get no bigger. A so mi know the place curse,' he said.

By now the sun was setting and I sensed that the deacon was getting ready to run for the hills. There was no way I was going to be left alone in that place, so when a rotten tree branch fell into the bushes and caused a slight noise, we all gave each other a quick glance and were immediately off without a word.

The last I saw of the deacon, he was pedalling his bicycle like crazy up a steep hill with sweat running down his forehead.

# (BARELY) SURVIVING A JAMAICAN TAXI CAB RIDE

I should've known that this was going to be weird. The car was missing a headlight and I could hear the engine rattling long before it came around the corner. Still, when the taxi pulled up, I was happy, especially since it was more than 15 minutes late. The driver, however, was quite pleased with himself and boasted about how fast he had driven to get there 'on time'.

I had poked my head inside when the car stopped, and glanced at the driver. He was huge, with a big head. Because he was so tall, he had to hang his head just so he could fit inside. He reminded me of those clowns who squeeze themselves into tiny cars at the circus. For a moment, I thought about telling him this but, when I sat in the car and realised that he could perhaps crush me with his thumb, I decided against it. Anyway, off we went. Our location: Spanish Town. Our destination: Kingston. Inside the car smelled like pine leaves and there was a furry cloth covering the seats. The windows were tinted and there was an air freshener in the shape of a tree, hanging from the rear-view mirror. There was a yellow cloth tucked under the emergency brake and the driver, who goes by the moniker 'Number 7', kept taking it up to wipe something or the other in the car.

We sat in silence until 'Number 7' pulled on to the Spanish Town bypass.

'You know a from when di govament claim 'bout dem a go build up dah road yah? A fool dem tek poor people fah, you know? All dem do a promise and den dem nuh do nothing,' he said, looking at me for a reaction. I made a gesture with my eyes and I guess this encouraged him to go on and on. 'All dem do a thief poor people money and go pan vacation wid dem wife and dem ting deh. Dem only care 'bout themselves,' he said.

Now, I'm sure that 'Number 7' went on further on the matter, but I was busy staring in front of me. 'Number 7' may be a good conversationalist, but his driving skills leave much to be desired. And, that's putting it mildly. Every time the car in front of his slowed down, even a bit, 'Number 7' would go into a tirade about how 'these people take the driving ting as a play play ting.' I didn't interrupt his ranting.

We were at a stoplight near to the hospital and before the light even went on green, 'Number 7' started tooting his horn and shouting for the driver in front of him to move his something or the other.

At more than 90 kilometres an hour, 'Number 7' shot across the bridge on his way to the Mandela Highway. What bothered me most was that while he pressed his foot on the accelerator, he remained calm, almost nonchalant about the whole affair. Meanwhile, I was sweating profusely and holding on tight to the fabric on my seat. My eyes were wide when I looked at him and said, as calmly as I could, 'You can take your time, you know, I'm not really in a rush.' Much to my consternation, this had little effect on 'Number 7', who now decided to strike up a conversation about the police.

**'Every time dem waan seize man cyar. Is like dem nuh waan do nothing else.** As dem hold you and realise dat you nuh have no insurance, dem waan tek weh yuh cyar. Is what happen to dem people yah?' he said. I wasn't able to give a response. My eyes were glued to a woman ahead of us crossing the road with a baby in her arms. She was, by now, directly in front of us, and 'Number 7' showed no signs of slowing the car down any time soon. I was silent, but in my head I was screaming, 'Lawd have mercy!'

Luckily, 'Number 7' swung the car around the woman in the nick of time and then made some comment about 'dem people yah who love run crass di road when dem see people a come.'

I was really in no mood to argue with a burly man, but couldn't help telling him that he could have slowed down a bit sooner when he noticed that the woman was crossing the road. I should have anticipated his response.

'No man! You haffi shake dem up. Dem galang like is fi dem road. Dem fi know dat is cyar and truck man run road.'

I didn't respond. There was little point, really.

By now, we were on Spanish Town Road. I remembered a newspaper article I had read about a week earlier which said that this road was a major crash spot last year.

I glanced at my watch and tried to convince myself that I would be at my destination and away from this maniac in only a few minutes.

'You see how di young bwoy win di competition? Yes man! Di woman dem gwaan like dem waan tek over everyting. Mi glad how di youth put har inna har place,' he said.

I saw myself hurtling toward the back of a truck and whispered a prayer for the preservation of my soul after my impending death. With only one eye open, I breathed a sigh of relief as the car swung around the truck, missing it by mere inches.

'Dem company yah dat a redundancy di people dem now. Wah you really think a gwaan?' He didn't give me a chance to respond. 'Is pure politics! All dem waan do is keep di people dem inna poverty. Marcus Garvey done tell dem,' he said, while barely missing the tail of a dog that ran across the road.

'Di two phone company dem inna tings wid dem one another. People nuh realise dat di two a dem a work wid dem one another fi mek more money off di poor people dem,' said 'Number 7'.

Ironically, his phone rang soon after and I wondered how much worse he could possibly drive, while distracted by a phone call. Luckily, he didn't accept the call and mumbled something about his babymother and money. I didn't care. I could see my destination now and, as the car came to a screeching halt, I thanked him and the heavens above for my survival.

I hopped out of the car and watched as 'Number 7', in his mobile death machine, shot down the road and out of sight.

# A JAMAICAN TAXI RIDE IN LONDON

While standing at a corner on a cool, misty morning in London, a black Vauxhall motor car pulled up in front of me. A yellow sign on top read 'taxi'. I wanted to get to Brixton, so I hopped in. The driver was an overweight man with caramel complexion. His face was round and he had a receding hairline. He had a slight beard and was wearing a grey shirt with a pair of weathered khaki pants. He seemed to be in his early 60s. 'Where to?' he said with a deep, raspy voice, before taking a sip of a steaming hot beverage in a paper cup he was holding.

I told him my destination and he turned to look at me. 'You is a Jamaican?' he asked. I responded, 'Yeah man,' and he let out a raucous chuckle. 'Mi was waiting on the 'yeah man'! Hee Hee!' he laughed. 'Mi know seh from you is a Jamaican you would say dat,' he said, still chuckling.

As the driver pulled the car on to the highway, he told me his name was Tony and that he is from Kitson Town in St. Catherine. 51 years ago, however, he moved to the United Kingdom in search of a better life, and today his home is in Brixton. 'Mi leave Jamaica and come here in 1956! You see how long mi deh here? Dat a when you daddy born young bwoy!' he snickered. 'Yes man, mi come here pan di ship when mi was 13 years old. Mi come stay wid mi uncle who was living here for some time,' Tony said. The plastic lid of the cup he was drinking from was resting on his leg. He took it up, glanced at his rear view mirror and then threw the lid through the window. He went back to talking as if nothing had happened.

'Yes. When mi come here mi was a likkle bwoy but because I was begging a place with my uncle I had was to find some work and do. Anyway, I had was to tell lie dat mi was actually 17 so I could get an apprentice work with a carpenter. So mi stay there fi a few years and learn the trade. After a while mi move out pan mi own and start make more money,' Tony said.

I asked him what he thought of England when he first arrived.

'Well, any Jamaican will tell you dat when you just come here to live you don't like it. It nuh nice because it so different from what you used to back home. Mi couldn't find nuh enjoyment in England when mi just come. All when Christmas time come it was depressing. When mi a grow up inna Jamaica when Christmas coming it was a big thing. Mama used to give we one slice a cake and cocoa and it was a big thing. Mi used to love dem ting deh! When mi come here mi lock up inside and

cyaan do anything. Mi cry whole day,' said Tony.

'Inna Jamaica we would look forward fi go a dance wid coconut bow a cover di sound box dem. Hee Hee! Mi love memba dem something deh!' Tony laughed.

'We woulda boogy inna di likkle nightclub dem pan Young Street and go out a road go drink a waters when we ready. But when you reach a England is a different ting! Not a enjoyment!' he said.

Tony explained that after living in England for several years, he eventually got accustomed to that nation's norms and has become quite at home there.

'When you just come it nuh nice but when you know that you coming here because you want to make a good life then you just ignore the negative feelings and eventually they will pass. Today, mi just as comfortable here as mi was back inna Jamaica,' said Tony.

'There is good life to live here in England you know, but you have to work hard for it. Life so far from you yard is a struggle but if you strong you will make it.'

I asked Tony what was the hardest thing to adjust to. 'Is when mi come here mi really realise dat mi is a black man. When mi in Jamaica I was just a regular youth because we never see skin colour but when I come here I realise quick. I used to go to people house to do carpenter work and dem turn mi back and say dem don't want any black people in dem house. Yes man!' Tony's eyebrows went skyward as he spoke.

'But as a Jamaican I know better than to make that bother me. I just carry on working hard until I could start my own company. Mi do very well too. Mi have four children born and grow here. All of them go university and have good jobs now. I own my own house and everything. Is just because I retire why I decide to drive taxi just to pass the time. I like it too. You able to meet plenty people,' he said.

Now much of what Tony said to me in the confines of that small black taxi in London could not have been published here. Suffice it to say that he still remembers all the uniquely Jamaican swear words and puts them to use with alarming frequency. Indeed, his authentic pronunciation of the famous Jamaican 'B' words was impressive, 51 years after he left Jamaica. I asked him about this. 'Whoi! All mi friend dem always ask mi dat! Even mi white friend dem. Dem always ask mi why mi cyaan learn fi chat better. But is alright, mi nuh want nuh accent. Mi is a Jamaican and is so we talk. Is mi language,' he said, with a nod.

Tony has no family left in Jamaica. He said they have all died. His wife and children all live in England. He said he's living a good life and is glad he didn't run back to Jamaica during his first unhappy years in England.

'Let mi tell you something young bwoy. You cannot judge a place when you nuh spend any time there. When I come here it was because times was hard in Jamaica. I know I couldn't leave just because I didn't like it. People who just come here will tell you dat it nuh nice but there is life to live here if you stick it out.'

Of the happenings back in Jamaica, Tony had this to say.

'I follow the news in Jamaica same way. Bwoy it distress mi. We have the the best, decent people in Jamaica yet we a shoot and chop up one another over nothing at all. Is time we stop dem ting deh now. Di world don't have nuh time fi people like dat. We have so much good tings and we need fi realise it and be thankful. The weather in Jamaica must be the best in the world and the jerk pork and music too. Lawd, if you only know how mi miss di life inna Jamaica!' Tony said, his eyes drifting off.

With these words, I arrived at my destination. I felt that I had made a new friend and bade the talkative old man goodbye with a handshake. When I got out of the car and closed the door behind me, Tony drove off slowly, but not before sticking his head through the window and giving the signature Jamaican farewell, 'Likkle more!'

With that, Tony the taxi driver disappeared.

# LOVER'S LEAP

Now if you're the hopeless romantic type, then the legend behind the popular spot called Lover's Leap in St. Elizabeth is probably high on your list of favourite stories. We've all heard one version or another of the tale. Two slaves who fell madly in love, jumping to their death to avoid behind torn apart by their wicked masters. A more sappy love story would be hard to find and many people travel from all over the world just to visit the spot where the dreamy-eyed slaves supposedly jumped from.

But as in all things, there are the non-believers, and as was to be expected, their view of the whole affair is a little

more, well, colourful. So I found out on a recent trip to Lover's Leap when I met up with one unassuming cynic with more than a mouthful to say.

I got to the spot about 3 o'clock on a warm afternoon and there were a few other people there just walking or standing around. I was minding my own business, looking over the cliff when suddenly I heard a voice behind me. 'You can walk down deh you know.' I turned around to face a slim man with a unique smile. He was wearing a black cap and a yellow shirt. 'Yes man. Just follow a little road around the side and you can reach right down to the sea,' the fellow said, walking closer to me. He wobbled slightly as he walked and squinted to keep the sun out of his eyes. I thought he made a funny picture. 'Yes man. I live around here now for more than 47 years and I see all kinda people go and come,' he said. 'You just have to follow the road and go right down,' he said pointing to the water.

'So tell me something. You believe all a dat?' he queried. I asked him what he was talking about. 'Dat story what dem tell about the slave and har man. 'Bout dem chuck off inna water fi love.' Before I could answer, he continued. 'Foolishness! Damn foolishness! Listen to me, nothing nuh go so! Nobody nah go jump from yah so. You think dem a idiot?'

He was shouting now and I started to wonder if he was blaming me for the story. 'Dem only tell people dat. But from mi born mi never yet hear 'bout anybody a jump because dem in love. Dem wouldn't do that. Afta dem nuh fool fool. What I believe happen is dat dem did stand up at the edge of the cliff and a strong breeze blow, and blow dem off inna di sea! Now dat make more sense,' he said, shaking his head.

'Is either that or dem did lick dem foot pan a stone and tumble over.'

Just then, a tall, slender man wearing spectacles walked up to us.

'Howdy, howdy,' he said to me and handed a cup filled with a pungent, clear liquid to the man I was speaking with. 'Hold dis Lee. Mine you drop off though. You might haffi chain up youself,' he said and walked away.

Now that I knew his name, I tried to get away. 'Alright Lee, I'll talk to you later,' I said and tried to slip away.

But Lee would have none of it. 'Look yah man. You is a scientist?' he asked. 'Er, no,' I said, realising that I was trapped. 'Well, I woulda like one scientist fi come down yah, for up to now I cannot find a john crow nest inna di bush,' he said. I scratched my head and wondered how the conversation had taken such a sudden and unexpected turn.

'Mi a run up and down round yah since mi a lilly bwoy and always see john crow. But I can never find him nest! A so mi know seh john crow have sense. Him know how fi hide him nest!' he said, looking quite intense. 'Yes man. Mi always can find di screech owl nest but neva di john crow nest,' he said.

'I know this place well. I live around here for nearly 50 years. The sea rough though. You cannot swim down there. My uncle drowned when mi was a bwoy and from dat mi nuh too tarry near di water,' he said.

'Mi used to go fishing, but the water get more dangerous since recent. The wave dem get stronger and now it nuh mek any sense fi go near di water,' Lee said.

He paused for a moment and turned around. A small wedding party had just arrived at the spot to take pictures. The groomsmen, all dressed in black suits with bow ties seemed to be having fun looking over at the water, more than 1,500 feet below. The bridesmaids were on the other side of the hill and most of them seemed scared to look over the edge.

'You can imagine, dem actually jump off dis!' said one of the younger men, his eyes wide. 'Bwoy dem mussi did really in love fi do dat! Di girl must did hot!'

'Foolishness!' shouted Lee from out of nowhere. I saw my chance and walked away. The last I saw of Lee, he was asking a frightened looking woman in a bouffant white wedding dress if she believed anybody would have been stupid enough to dive to their death in the name of love.

---

*Note to Lisa: It was like being on top of the world with you. Thanks again!*

# THE DUPPY WOMAN

The duppy woman ran straight at me with her hands in the air! I thought to myself, all right, this is it, the duppy inside her is about to jump into me and I'll have to spend the rest of my life being called the duppy man. But just as I braced myself for the impact, someone whispered in my ear, 'She come to shake your hand.' A tad red in the face, I managed a smile, but must admit that I was still a bit nervous as I shook her hand. I mean, it's not every day I meet a duppy woman. A few witches, maybe, but never a real life duppy woman.

But let me tell you how I got to be in the company of a self-proclaimed duppy woman in the first place. Carrie is a middle-aged woman from Kellits in Clarendon who now lives in New Hall, St. Ann. Her claim to fame is that she has been set upon by one brute of a duppy called Wenticko, every year, during crop time, for more than 18 years.

The story is that she caught a man in Kellits fiddling around with a pig in a most peculiar way. She supposedly raised an alarm and the pig-lover set a hex on her. According to the people of Kellits, some of whom I met a few weeks back, the duppy has done all kinds of things with Carrie. He supposedly has folded her up and put her in a drawer, rolled her up a hill and even put her at the top of a hundred foot tree. But was all this true? Only one way to find out, so

photographer Ian Allen and I went in pursuit of the duppy woman at her new home in New Hall, St. Ann.

Now, if you don't know your way around, New Hall is not an easy place to find. But we quickly realised that Carrie was quite popular and this was going to make our job a lot easier.

'You know Carrie?' I hollered to an elderly man smoking a pipe on his veranda.

'Carrie? You mean di one weh Wenticko did a follow?' he shouted back.

And so it went on, we drove around asking for Carrie, the woman 'followed' by Wenticko, and eventually arrived right at her home. It was an old house with a rusting zinc roof. A little spooky, but not as bad as I expected.

Sharon, a neighbour, poked her head through a window of

her home. "Can I help you?" she inquired.

'We're here to see Carrie,' I said.

'Oh, yes she inside. Carrie! Carrie! Somebody here to see you!' she shouted.

This was it. There was no turning back now. I expected to see a strapping woman, perhaps wearing a triangular hat and some pointed shoes, but to my surprise, a little pleasant looking woman came strolling merrily down the hill. She ran right up to me and extended her arm. When I realised what she was doing, I shook her hand.

'How are you please?' she asked with a smile. 'Er...ah...fine,' I said, caught off guard by how normal she seemed.

So were all the stories true? We got right into the matter. 'Oh yes man. Me is di duppy woman. Mi nuh business what people want to say. Dem say mi shouldn't call myself so, but I don't mind. Is who mi is,' she said with a smile.

'So do you remember the first time that Wenticko possessed you?' I asked.

'Yes man. Is not me even catch di man with the pig. Is somebody else, a little boy name Junie. So di man really set the science pan Junie,' she said.

'So how did it reach you?' I queried.

'Well Junie did have a goat tie up inna di field. Him did suppose to go for it, but him did sick. So him ask mi fi go for di goat for him. Is when mi go fi di goat dat the blow reach me,' she said, rubbing her temple. 'What you mean "the blow reach you"?' I asked.

'I mean dat is when the science dat suppose to reach Junie, reach me instead. Mi just knock out and next thing mi know mi inna di air, like how dem carry coffin,' Carrie remembered.

The soft-spoken woman said she has got so accustomed to Wenticko over the years, that she is no longer afraid. 'Is crop time now, and dat mean him might come again, but mi nuh fraid. Mi not even know when it happen. Is like him take over mi body, so mi not even conscious. Mi nuh fret 'bout it bredda,' she said.

As a rooster made some puzzling sounds in the background, I asked Carrie what were some of the things that Wenticko has done to her. 'Him put gravel inna mi food, put mi up inna tree top and burn up mi foot.' She showed us the scars on her legs.

Carrie said neighbours have taken her all over, trying to rid her of the curse. 'Mi go church and the pastor run mi. Him say is me doing it. Mi go madda woman and she bathe mi inna all kinda something. But nothing nuh work.'

Carrie moved to New Hall about a year ago. 'Do the people here bother you?' I asked.

'No man, dem take care of me. Dem nuh badda mi at all.' Sure enough, we spoke with several neighbours who said they had no problem with Carrie living there. 'If di duppy deh pan her den him nah go trouble anybody else,' said Miss Gatty who lives across the road.

Indeed, Carrie is happy in New Hall. You see, the sporadically possessed belle moved there to be with the man she loves, one Ustas Kelly. Yes, theirs is a pure love. Ustas told us that duppy or no duppy, Carrie is his woman.

Fresh from his field, with machete in hand, Ustas explained why he wasn't scared of being with a woman who calls herself 'the duppy woman'. 'Is somebody pickney same way. Is one man mi fear and is God. Mi nuh fraid a dem evil things. Wenticko can't chat to mi, for me and him ah nuh quabs!' he shouted. Ustas said he boiled some bushes and gave to his woman earlier this year, and so Wenticko has so far stayed away. He pointed to a table in the front yard, on which several bottles and some weeds were placed.

'That is not a obeah table, it's a Zion table. It will keep weh di bugga!' Ustas professed. So that was that. Our visit with the duppy woman had come to an end. Back to Kingston.

Alone, I hope!

# WONDERS OF BATH, ST. THOMAS

With the Rasta man grinning broadly in the background, the chubby woman in the tiny bathing suit hopped on one foot, raised her hands to the heavens and shouted, 'It's a miracle, one time I couldn't do this. I couldn't even walk or talk!'

Now under normal circumstances, the woman's antics would have raised a few eyebrows, and frankly would have had me searching for the exit. But where I was standing at Bath Fountain in St. Thomas, it's an everyday occurrence.

You see, this is no ordinary place. Locals say that the steaming hot water coming from the hills is the most powerful medicine on earth and can heal any ailment from cancer to leprosy. There are famous tales of hundreds of persons who have been healed by the mystical powers of the potent water. Limp feet have apparently sprung to life and darkened eyes have suddenly seen the light. A miraculous place it seemed indeed! So photographer Norman Grindley and I wasted no time as we headed off to the aquatic wonder to see the light for ourselves, and to find out from the people who live there just what is the secret behind the powers of Bath Fountain.

The famous fountain is the star attraction in the community called Bath. Everybody we talked with had a story to tell about somebody who was healed there or of the history of the fountain.

One straggler thought it fit to go into great detail about his once flaccid extremity that now springs to action with great alacrity at the slightest prompting.

Needless to say, I got more information than I would have liked. About a half mile from the bath we came across a dreadlocked man who was standing behind a bamboo hut. There were coconuts hanging all around and a sign gave the name of the hut as 'Black Beads Shop'.

We asked the man, who gave his name as Adelaja, about the mysterious fountain. 'Well is a great healing you know, Bingi. You want to see seh is jus the works of the Most High inna dat place. People pass me right here on the way up to the fountain with crutches and pass me back going down without them. So is just the healing of the Creator,' the man said.

We pressed him to tell us what he knew of the history of the fountain. 'Well you know Bingi is a slave did really run away into the hills you know. Him did have a sore foot and stay up there for ten days and get healed. So when him go back home him tell the other slave dem 'bout the water. Dem did have sore foot too. So when dem go and get heal, then is so the whole place really get discover, you know, Bingi,' he said.

We bid Adelaja farewell and headed further up the hill to find the fountain.

We got to a dead end where about a dozen dreadlocked men were standing around.

'Greetings in the name of His Majesty. Anything you want, you get. Anything you have, we heal. The water heal everything except bad mind!' shouted a man wearing a torn pair of shorts, who later gave his name as Ras Desmond. We told him our mission. 'Well I going to take you up to meet Jah Truci, him is the mayor of the river,' he said. All the other men nodded in agreement and Jah Truci suddenly seemed like a worshipped being.

(c) 2006 The Gleaner Co. Ltd.

I was a bit taken aback.

We followed Ras Desmond up a very narrow path that went straight up into the hills. We walked for about ten minutes before we heard the sound of rushing water. We could now see the water. There was steam rising from the water as it bubbled out of the hills. There were six more dreadlocked men attending to persons in the river. Ras Desmond led us right into the water. 'Wait here let me call the mayor,' he said.

A few minutes later, he returned with a man wearing only a pair of underpants and a smile. It was Jah Truci. 'Yes, greetings my brother. Welcome to the most powerful place on Jah earth,' he said. We asked the river mayor to tell us about the fountain. 'Well is a slave by the name of Jacob Stevenstene had leprosy and came up here for ten days and was healed. When the bakra massa find out about it then the place just get famous. Everybody start come here for healing and is so it continue from then until now,' the man said.

'Well I man deh here for more than 20 years and help give healing to hundreds of people. I see this water cure bad allergies, sinus, cancer, everything. Even cripple people come up here and walk again. Is a precious ointment for the people. It really powerful, spiritually and physically,' Jah Truci went on.

Just then, a woman with curly grey hair walked up to us. She had an American accent.

'Hi. Look at me if you want to know about the power of the water,' she said. The woman said that she lives in Philadelphia and was involved in a major car crash in 1995 that left her blind in one eye and partially paralysed. She said a friend took her to Jamaica in 1996 and she visited Bath. 'Look at me now! I can sing and do everything. My eyes are working fine and I can walk again!' she said, jumping up and down. The woman said that a major university in the U.S. is working on a publication about her miraculous healing.

Jah Truci smiled in agreement. 'The dawta come here every year

since that and get her treatment. Is a blessing,' he said.

'When you get treatment all you have to do is have a jelly and relax. Keep cool and everything will heal itself. Is the power of the ancestors in the water. That's why the water is so hot coming out of the hills. Is just the natural spirits,' Jah Truci said.

'If you have a problem just come to the river. Jah mek it for everybody to get a healing and to get a blessing. Is just the powers of the Most High for the people to enjoy.'

99

# THE GOOD LIFE
# IN PORT ROYAL

My Knees started wobbling something fierce! I heard a shuffling noise behind me and I whipped around just in time to see something move in the bushes of the graveyard. My eyebrows went north in a haste and a trickle of sweat fell on to my nose. The pain in my chest told me this was it and my eyes started scanning the grounds for the best place to spend eternity.

Thankfully, however, I lived to tell the tale. Alas, it wasn't the boogie man after all. The noise in the bushes was caused by nothing more than a stray dog which had wandered into the graveyard in hot pursuit of a plump mongoose.

Perhaps I should explain why I was in the middle of the old graveyard in the first place.

You see, photographer Norman Grindley and I were in Port Royal recently and heard about the tale of the 'undead soldiers'. Yes, it's as creepy as it sounds.

Legend has it that some of the soldiers buried in the old Royal Navy cemetery are, let's say, a bit frisky even now, centuries after their death. Some say the spirits of the soldiers, many of whom died in battle or of the then dreaded yellow fever, lurk around the cemetery and the streets of Port Royal at night in search of their old navy ships or for longlost friends.

Now this isn't exactly the kind of thing you hear everyday, so perhaps against better judgement, we went there to check the place out for ourselves.

The cemetery was itself almost buried in bushes. Large, prickly plants covered most of the graves. There was a monument with a rusty, old anchor on top of it.

# Most of the graves had concrete crosses on top of them and these, coupled with the bushes, made the scene more eerie

- as if it wasn't eerie enough just being a graveyard. The tombstones mostly described navy officers who died in their early 20s in battle. Some died in the 19th century, others in the early 1900s.

It was easy to see why this place would have spawned the legend of the undead soldiers, because it was still bright out, early afternoon, and to tell you the truth, the place was giving me the heebie jeebies. But after spending some time there without one ghost showing his face, we realised that perhaps it was rest day in the afterlife, so we left and decided to check out the rest of Port Royal.

Now most people know the history of Port Royal and that it was once known as the wickedest place on earth. From what we heard, it is now one of the most peaceful places in the country. We wanted to find out if this was true and how the residents pulled it off.

We drove around for a bit, looking around. There was a strong smell of fish and a couple men were staggering out of bars with bottles in their hands. A spirited bunch.

We met up with Aunt May at her little shop called 'May's Grocery'. Aunt May is 84 years old and well respected in Port Royal. Everyone calls her Aunt May or just aunty and we were told she is like a mother to the entire community.

We found the bright-eyed golden ager shooting the breeze in front of her shop. She was resting on a chair and chatting with a smartly dressed bloke who wore a pair of rather dark sunglasses.

'Howdi do?' the woman greeted us as we pulled up beside her. She gave a hearty chuckle. We told her why we were there and the woman chuckled again.

'Boy, you couldn't find a better place than Port Royal. In fact, I have travelled all over the world. Norway, England, Canada and the United States and I have never come across a more peaceful, friendly place than right here. And I am 84 years old!' Aunt May rubbed her forehead as she spoke. 'Some people don't believe that we are so close to Kingston yet we are so different. To tell you the truth, I don't even pass Harbour View anymore. Right here you can sit out on the street until three o'clock in the morning and nobody trouble you. You sleep with your windows and doors wide open and you don't feel any way.'

The fellow with the dark glasses chimed in. Aunt May called him Kelly. 'I am 72 and I agree. I travel out and come back. This is where I was born and I never see a place nice like this one,' the lanky fellow said.

I asked the two community stalwarts just how the residents managed to keep the place so peaceful.

'They say it's all the fish we eat. Hee Hee!' Aunt May quipped. 'It's really just how you live with each other. Right here we live like one jolly family. I am like the aunty to everybody. Once you live good then you don't have a problem. Nobody going to trouble you,' Aunt May said.

The pair told us that tourists visit the community all the time to gawk at the historic structures, but not many persons pay attention to the residents of the area who, she said, are an example to the rest of the country. 'Yes you have the Giddy House and the canons, but it's the way of life in Port Royal that is the real marvel,' she said with a glimmer in her eye.

We walked around with Aunt May and she introduced us to what seemed like everyone in the community. And by name! We had a grand time with the jolly folks of Port Royal and found it to be a most welcoming community. One fisherman, fresh from sea, summed up life in the community best.

'We nuh have nuh time fi war wid wi one another. It ago tek weh time from di fish an di liquor!'

# PENLYNE CASTLE

It was only a matter of time. One last bang and the vehicle would go no more. It needed a rest at least, so photographer Norman Grindley and I hopped out to look around and to figure out just where exactly we were. We had started out on quite a casual drive to Portland, but soon found ourselves crawling up the Blue Mountains. We had lost all track of civilisation some ways back, and now seemed to be in the middle of nowhere.

When the vehicle screeched to a halt, it sent a cloud of dust right into my nostrils. I coughed and struggled to make out my surroundings. There was complete silence, but the view was spectacular. There were giant trees all around and we were so high up that it seemed like we were on top of the entire island. I couldn't see anyone, but there were a few homes with zinc and board fences along the way. I heard a shuffling noise and realised that someone was coming up the road behind us.

When the dust had settled, I realised that it was a short schoolboy dressed in khaki and carrying a knapsack on his back. When he was close, I asked him where we were.

'It name Penlyne Castle, Sir,' he said, and continued walking.

So now we knew where we were, but there didn't seem to be anyone else to speak with. Nothing seemed to be going on. We decided to start walking up the hill to see if there was anything further north, though the piercing silence left me less than hopeful. After a few minutes of hiking, I spotted a lone figure in the distance. He was a dreadlocked fellow with very dark skin and a muscular body. He must have been in his mid-50s and was standing near some green bushes and a small tree. He was hunched over and seemed to be concentrating on something at his feet, but from where we were, I couldn't make out what it was.

As we got closer, the man turned to face us. 'Hello,' he said, dryly. We greeted the man and told him we were interested in learning more about the place. He chuckled. 'Well, you not going to find much round here in Penlyne Castle right now. For is only pure coffee farmer like me live around here. Most man deh a bush right yah now still,' he said, looking me up and down. I asked him why he wasn't 'at bush' like his fellow farmers.

'Well, me is a man do my thing different. Mi go from earlier and come in and cool off. Right now mi just a catch some water and mi a go back,' he said.

It was then that I noticed that the thing at the man's feet that he was concentrating on was a small plastic bottle. There was crystal clear water trickling from the ground and the man was collecting some of it in his bottle. 'This water is pure Blue Mountain spring water. You can bathe inna it and drink it. Is God make this water, so it must be good. Nuh badda feel seh because it a come from inna di ground it dirty. No man, is clean water,' he persisted.

He finally gave his name as Joe, and explained that most of the people who lived in the community were well experienced coffee farmers. 'Even the young people dem that coming up take to di farming. Right now is what most people do around here. Is it dem use to make a living,' he said.

Joe was interrupted when he realised that his bottle was full and he bent over to pick it up. 'Well, I gone, you hear? I have to go dig off, for mi nuh done do what mi was doing. So you take care and all the best,' he said as he walked away with a smile on his face. But before disappearing, he told us of a shop a few more feet up the hill where he said we would be able to find more people to talk with. We headed in that direction immediately. Soon we could hear the faint sound of a radio and eventually we came across a tiny shop painted blue. It was a concrete structure but looked like it was made of wood. There were a few young boys playing marbles in the dirt just at the entrance to the shop. We passed them and walked inside. There, we met Pauline, the shopkeeper. Her skin was fair and she had piercings in the most exciting places. She was a chubby woman and seemed pleasant enough. We greeted her and asked about life in Penlyne Castle.

'Well, I don't know what to tell you. It very quiet and sometimes boring. But we meet a lot of people who come here to climb and hike. Dem come from all over and so dem will come and stop and refresh themselves. Last week I meet a man from Germany. Yes, mi chile! Him say him want to married mi off, but mi tell him say him too ugly fi me. Hee hee!' Pauline seemed about to tumble over with laughter.

'Mi not going to married him, for mi not even know him. Maybe if him come and spend some time, but afta mi nuh idiot!' she said, looking cross.

'But Penlyne Castle is a little quiet place. I used to live in Kingston and since I come up here mi nuh have any more stress. Here, nobody nuh trouble you. Everybody live good.

Di only thing you have to worry about is landslide and duppy. Di weather always cool and you always can find sinting fi eat. Dat is why so much people come from all over the world. This place blessed,' she said.

# THE SCOTT TOWN MONSTER

There's something strange lurking in the bushes in Scott Town, Manchester and it has the whole town abuzz. It's unlike anything anyone there has ever seen before. The creature has been spotted in Maas Helton's banana field more than once and now the shaken man is afraid to leave his bed at night.

'Di first time me see di sinting, mi just took off! Mi nah go lay lay and mek it nyam mi raw!' Mass Helton said.

He's a short fellow with graying hair and he has noticeable trouble pronouncing the letter 'v', but his memory of the first time he encountered the mysterious beast is impeccable.

'It was around 3 o'clock inna di morning. Mi decide fi get up early and go inna mi field. Mi and mi dog go round a di back and mi only see when the dog walk off. So mi stand up one side fi see where him a go. Den mi hear one digging noise and mi look and see something a dig up di banana tree. Mi frighten now and bend down behind one bush and a watch. Mi see di dog walk up to di creature and den mi just hear whoo, whoo! When mi hear dat mi gallop weh left all di dog! Dem bwoy out a road say mi too fraid, but mi nuh care!' Maas Helton shouted.

He said the creature had four long and narrow legs like a goat and a long face with an obvious snout. It was furry and about twice the size of a large dog.

'It front foot hab on four claw and it move very fast. If you quint too fast then you miss it,' he said.

Now news of the strange animal spread across the community like wildfire and soon, plans for a public execution were put in place.

At the crack of dawn the next day, almost everyone from the community turned up at Maas Helton's home, wielding machetes and carrying torches. 'Dem come say dem ready fi kill di brute. Everybody ready fi chop him up. Anyhow dem did ketch him, a murder,' Maas Helton said.

## But they didn't catch the creature and Miss Eva, who walked up to join Maas Helton, knows why.

'Him nuh love noise. Di creature only come out a night time. My cousin see it down by Miss Mama garden. Anyhow him hear noise, him dig off,' she said.

Miss Eva is a strapping woman who had a bunch of clothes pegs attached to the bottom of her blouse. She said she was washing clothes at the back of her house when she heard us talking about the beast.

'People say dem afraid since the beast deh 'bout. But I not afraid. I not locking up myself inside the house. I must go church and no devil will stop me from go church! Mi nuh fear no foe! Him haffi go nyam mi!' she said adamantly.

Now most people who live in the community are farmers and are more than a bit agitated that this beast has been running around in their fields and stealing pumpkins and melons. So now the men of Scott Town have devised what they think is an ingenious plan to catch the strange creature. Their plan is to make some giant traps and place them on everyone's property. If that doesn't work, then they all plan to spend the night in the bushes and wait for the first sign of the beast. 'We going to use some melon and catch him. Him always a trouble people melon and plantain. We going to put out some melon and wait pon him. We haffi ketch him!' Maas Helton said.

By now a crowd had gathered and everyone was talking about how they could possibly catch the beast. I asked Maas Helton what kind of creature he thought it was.

'Well mi see it and mi really nuh know. A man tell mi dat it could be a kangaroo.

Another man tell mi dat is a duppy. Right yah now mi nuh really certain. All mi know is that any day mi spot it again, mi a go dig off,' he said.

Miss Jane, an elderly woman wearing a cap, spectacles and a pair of running shoes, walked up to join us. She too had her fair share to say on the matter. 'These are the last days! That is why all a dem creature yah leggo pan di earth. God is calling his people! Repent!' she said to nobody in particular.

This silenced the others for a few seconds and then Maas Helton spoke up again.

'Di creature look like him have relation with the dog dem, for when him come round, the dog dem nuh mek nuh noise. Mi have four big dog and none a dem ever make noise when di creature come around. Is like him hypnotise dem wid him eye dem,' he said. The others seemed to agree. Dwayne, Maas Helton's son, chimed in. 'Yes! Is like him have some kinda magic. More time him look like him can disappear. Mi nuh know what it is, but it must be evil!' he said.

As evening approached in the rural town, everyone scattered, each heading to his own home. It was to be another night of waiting in fear. Waiting for another sign of the Scott Town monster.

112

# ONE LOVE IN SHIRLEY CASTLE

The dreadlock man walked into the shop and up to the counter. 'Miss Grace! Gimme two pound a pig tail deh!' I thought it a bit curious that he would be partaking of the swine. Then again, there was a church down the road that had only two members and according to residents, it rains in the community every single day, so I should have known that Shirley Castle was no ordinary place.

Yes, photographer Norman Grindley and I were in Shirley Castle district, hidden deep in the hills of Portland. And when I say hidden, I mean really hidden.

Only about 200 persons live in the community which is covered with fog for about nine hours of every day. It's so high up in the mountains that you feel as if you're in heaven looking down on the world.

I guess sensing my unease, the dreadlocked bloke introduced himself. 'How you gentlemen doing?' he said rather eloquently. 'My name is Zeke, good to see the gentleman dem passing through. We is all one Jamaican,' he said with a smile.

Zeke was dressed in black from head to toe. It was raining, so he even had a black plastic bag on his head to keep dry. He was wearing an improvised raincoat that looked more like a cape. I chuckled to myself when I first saw him, thinking he looked like a comic book character. He was, however,

wielding a machete, so I quickly stifled the laugh. We were in the only shop in all of Shirley Castle district. Miss Grace, the proprietor, was relaxing behind the counter. She wore an unusually thick pair of glasses and a green dress. Upon Zeke's request, the middle-aged woman retreated into a back room.

Zeke told us that he was a coffee farmer and that most of the men in the community did the same kind of work. 'Dat is what we do round here. We grow di best coffee in the world right here,' he said, water dripping from his plastic hat onto his water boots.

By then, two other men came up a hill and into the small shop. They too were carrying machetes and wore water boots. They were soaking wet. 'Morning, morning. How unnu doing?' they asked as they walked by us. 'Miss Grace!

trust mi a pound a rice and some salt ting deh!' the taller of the two shouted. 'Ah coming to you!' Miss Grace shouted back.

The men joined us. They were Lennox and Milton. 'Bwoy, most people don't know 'bout Shirley Castle still, but trust me, is the nicest place to live,' Milton said. He was a pleasant fellow. He wore a rain drenched red shirt and his hands were covered with dirt.

'I wouldn't leave dis place fi nothing.' Milton said he had never been outside his community and saw no reason to ever venture out. 'Mi have everything mi need. Friend, food, mi farm, mi criss!' the 30-something-year-old said, causing the others to chuckle.

Lennox was more adventurous. Well, slightly. 'Mi go

Kingston one time when mi did falla mi neighbour go pick up him daughter a di airport. Afta dat mi seh mi naw go back massa. Too much noise and ting. Mi nuh inna it bawba!' he said, looking rather displeased by the memory.

Miss Grace had rejoined the group with Zeke's pig's tail and Lennox's 'salt ting'.

'Den Miss Grace, ah wah kinda fenkeh fenkeh piece a meat dis?' Lennox quipped as he examined the peculiar looking contents of a plastic bag the woman handed to him.

'Bwoy you fi have manners. You nuh see company deh yah. Nuh seh dem ting deh in front a di Kingston man dem. Look yah, don't mek mi get dark,' the woman responded, waving a fist at the frightened looking Lennox. 'So ... Sorry Miss Grace' he replied sheepishly.

Miss Grace turned to me. 'Now what you

need to know is dat the people in Shirley Castle live like one family. Nothing like crime here. The last time a policeman come up here was 12 years ago,' she said. I chuckled, thinking it was a joke. 'Ah wah you a laugh 'bout? Is a serious ting. Police only come here when dem a check a friend or something.

No crime or anything up dis side,' Miss Grace finished, inducing nods of agreement from the men. 'Dat is why mi naw go back a Kingston,' Lennox stated, as if justifying his decision.

'You know what else different 'bout dis place?' Miss Grace looked back at me. 'It rain here everyday!'

This brought shouts of approval from the others in the group. 'If is even for a minute, rain fall everyday. Dat's why mi tell you seh dis place is God blessed,' Lennox chimed in. Outside, a steady line of farmers were making their way from their fields. They all sheltered from the rain with huge leaves they cut off trees. Some used leaves off plantain trees, others used bushes. It was quite a sight when the group walked together. Even in the rain, each farmer managed to wave hello before passing by.

Miss Grace told us that just across the road, lived Mr. Bradshaw who was a highly respected Justice of the Peace. The group insisted that we go over to his home and speak with him. So we bid the friendly few farewell and headed across the road.

Knock, knock. We pounded on the gate. A short, stocky man appeared in the doorway.

'Yes, come in. Come along,' he said, smiling. Before we could get out a word, he extended his hand and offered us seats on his veranda. We told him we wanted to know a bit about the community. 'Well the main thing is that this is a very friendly, quiet place.

We all live like a family. I have been here all my life and I have never heard of any crime being committed here,' he said. Mr. Bradshaw confirmed that it rains almost every day in the community. The rain is the only source of water the residents have. There are no water pipes, only a spring and a large tank that collects rain water. But the friendly people of Shirley Castle don't seem to mind. Mr. Bradshaw said it best. 'We don't have many things that other communities have. But we all can't have everything. We have peace and love and so we are all alright.'

# REMEMBERING A FATHER'S LOVE

As far as I know there is only one person who has never missed a single edition of 'Roving with Lalah' since I started writing the feature almost two years ago. In fact, he saved a copy of every single article I've ever written. My dad would go around telling everyone he met that his son wrote a feature in the *Gleaner* and he was more proud of me than anyone has ever been. He passed away recently, so this week I honour him by dedicating his favourite weekly feature to him.

One Monday morning when I was about four years old, I jumped out of bed, expecting to see my mother standing over me, telling me to go get ready for school. But there was something different about this Monday morning.

When I opened my eyes I didn't see anyone. The room was empty and my ears hurt from the silence. Puzzled by this unexpected break in routine, I ran out of my bedroom, into the kitchen and looked from side to side. I couldn't find anyone, so like any self respecting four-year-old, I burst into tears. Not surprising to me, my father came running when he heard me cry out. He was all dressed and my brother and sister were with him. Both of them were wearing their school clothes and I realised that they were about to leave for school. I was in the first grade at the time, so normally I would've gone with them. I felt like I was being left out, so I cried even more, until my dad picked me up and kissed me on the cheek.

'It's ok, you and I are going to the country today,' he said in his calm, reassuring voice. I stopped crying immediately and my mom came and took me from him. 'I'm just going to take your brother and sister to school and come back for you,' he said, with a wink. That was the first of many days during my school years that my dad would keep me home from school so that we could spend more time together. In those days, I was just happy to be out of school, but now that I look back at the time I spent with my father, I realise how precious those days really were. We didn't do much on those days. Maybe we'd drive to the country or go get ice cream,

but no matter how simple those days were, they helped create some of the happiest memories I have of spending time with my father. I realised early that the effort and care that my dad put into raising his three children wasn't exactly customary. I remember when I was quite young, telling my friends at school about playing cricket and football with my dad and of him packing my lunch box every morning before he took me to school. I told them how he quit his job as a well-paid executive so that he could spend more time with his

wife and children. I was often met with surprised looks and at least a couple friends accused me of making up stories.

But that was my father. It was hard for me to go an entire day at school without mentioning him, because he was so involved in my life and the lives of my brother and sister. He would prepare our lunches, take us to school and then pick us up in the evenings. Because of that, all my friends knew him and I was always proud of talking about him. When he picked us up from school, we would go straight to my mom's office to pick her up from work. It was a routine that formed a big part of my life for many years and I can clearly remember my father telling me that it was important for all of us to go home together so that we could all have dinner at the same time. And so we did. For years, he would insist that we all sit

together every evening to have dinner. I wish he was here for me to thank him for that now. Because of the admiration that I felt for my father since I was very young, I grew up watching him very closely and tried my best to do everything exactly the way he did. He loved writing, so I started writing. He loved reading so I started reading everything I could find. He loved sports, so I started watching games with him.

Everything he did, I wanted to do and I think he knew that all three of his children were watching him very closely. This was a huge responsibility and one

that might have felt like a major burden for a lesser man. But believe me, my dad didn't falter once. We watched him and the care and compassion he showed to my mother and we learned what a marriage should be and how a real man treats the woman he loves. We watched him cook her meals, rub her feet, paint her toenails, hug her when she was sad and care for her when she was sick. We watched him kiss her every morning when he took her to work and we watched him rearrange his schedule just so he would have time to pick her up from work. All of this without a single complaint. My parents were married for more than thirty years, but my dad was so in love with my mother that whenever he talked about her, his face would light up like a teenager in love.

He was proud of his wife and his three children and would bring them up in almost every conversation he had. He carried our pictures with him in his wallet and was quick to pull them out in front of complete strangers if he felt that the occasion warranted it. By the time I was old enough

to understand the concept of friendship, I heard both my sister and brother refer to our dad as their best friend. Of course my mom did the same thing. It didn't take me long to realise why they felt that way and in no time I was going around telling everyone that my father was my best friend.

After all, he was the only person each of us knew that we could call on no matter what the problem was, and he would find a way to solve it. No matter what we did, he would not judge us and no matter how stupid we acted, he would never stop loving us. It was a blessing to have loved and lived with him for so many years. My only regret is that I did not have more time with him. Under his guidance I could have learned a lot more. But what he taught me during his life I will never forget and no matter how much time passes or how old I get, a part of me will always be that little boy sitting in the backseat of my father's car, looking up at him and thinking that he was just the greatest man God ever created.